THE TROPICAL
Series Editor
René Coste

General Editor, Livestock Volumes
Anthony J. Smith

Centre for Tropical Veterinary Medicine
University of Edinburgh

Livestock Production Systems

R Trevor Wilson

Bartridge Partners
Umberleigh

Macmillan Education
Between Towns Road, Oxford OX4 3PP
A division of Macmillan Publishers Limited
Companies and representatives throughout the world

ISBN 978 0 333 60012 2

First published 1995

Published in co-operation with the CTA (Technical
Centre for Agriculture and Rural Co-operation), P.O.B. 380,
6700 AJ Wageningen, The Netherlands

www.macmillan-africa.com

Cover photograph by A. J. Smith

Printed and bound in Malaysia

2015 2014 2013 2012 2011 2010 2009
12 11 10 9 8 7 6

Technical Centre for Agricultural and Rural Co-operation (ACP-EU)

The Technical Centre for Agricultural and Rural Co-operation (CTA) was established in 1983 under the Lomé Convention between the ACP (African, Caribbean and Pacific) Group of States and the European Union Member States.

CTA's tasks are to develop and provide services that improve access to information for agricultural and rural development, and to strengthen the capacity of ACP countries to produce, acquire, exchange and utilise information in these areas. CTA's programmes are organised around four principal themes: developing information management and partnership strategies needed for policy formulation and implementation; promoting contact and exchange of experience; providing ACP partners with information on demand; and strengthening their information and communication capacities.

CTA, Postbus 380, 6700 AJ Wageningen, The Netherlands.

Agency for Cultural and Technical Co-operation (ACCT)

The Agency for Cultural and Technical Co-operation, an intergovernmental organisation set up by the Treaty of Niamey in March 1970, is an association of countries linked by their common usage of the French language, for the purposes of co-operation in the fields of education, culture, science and technology and, more generally, in all matters which contribute to the development of its Member States and to bringing peoples closer together.

The Agency's activities in the fields of scientific and technical co-operation for development are directed primarily towards the preparation, dissemination and exchange of scientific and technical information, drawing up an inventory of and exploiting natural resources, and the socio-economic advancement of young people and rural communities.

Member countries: Belgium, Benin, Burkina Faso, Burundi, Canada, Central African Republic, Chad, Comoros, Congo, Côte d'Ivoire, Djibouti, Dominica, France, Gabon, Guinea, Haiti, Lebanon, Luxembourg, Mali, Mauritius, Monaco, Niger, Rwanda, Senegal, Seychelles, Togo, Tunisia, Vanuatu, Vietnam, Zaire.

Associated States: Cameroon, Egypt, Guinea-Bissau, Laos, Mauritania, Morocco, St Lucia.

Participating governments: New Brunswick, Quebec.

Titles in *The Tropical Agriculturalist* series

Sheep	ISBN 0-333-79881-3	Animal Health Vol.1	0-333-61202-7
Pigs	0-333-52308-3	Animal Health Vol.2	0-333-57360-9
Goats	0-333-52309-1	Warm-water	
Dairying	0-333-52313-X	Crustaceans	0-333-57462-1
Poultry	0-333-79149-5	Livestock Production	
Rabbits	0-333-52311-3	Systems	0-333-60012-6
Draught Animals	0-333-52307-5	Donkeys	0-333-62750-4
Ruminant Nutrition	0-333-57073-1	Camels	0-333-60083-5
Animal Breeding	0-333-57298-X	Tilapia	0-333-57472-9
Upland Rice	0-333-44889-8	Plantain Bananas	0-333-44813-8
Tea	0-333-54450-1	Coffee Growing	0-333-54451-X
Cotton	0-333-47280-2	Food Legumes	0-333-53850-1
Weed Control	0-333-54449-8	Cassava	0-333-47395-7
Spice Plants	0-333-57460-5	Sorghum	0-333-54452-8
Cocoa	0-333-57076-6	Cut Flowers	0-333-62528-5
The Storage of Food		Coconut	0-333-57466-4
Grains and Seeds	0-333-44827-8	Market Gardening	0-333-65449-8
Avocado	0-333-57468-0	Forage Husbandry	0-333-66856-1
Sugar Cane	0-333-57075-8	Oil Palm	0-333-57465-6
Maize	0-333-44404-3	Alley Farming	0-333-60080-0
Food Crops and		Chickpeas	0-333-63137-1
Drought	0-333-59831-8	Rubber	0-333-68355-2
Groundnut	0-333-72365-1	Livestock Behaviour,	
		Management and	
		Welfare	0-333-62749-0

Other titles published by Macmillan with CTA (*co-published in French by Maisonneuve et Larose*)

Animal Production in the Tropics and Subtropics	ISBN 0-333-53818-8
Coffee: The Plant and the Product	0-333-57296-3
The Tropical Vegetable Garden	0-333-57077-4
Controlling Crop Pests and Diseases	0-333-57216-5
Dryland Farming in Africa	0-333-47654-9
The Yam	0-333-57456-7

The Land and Life Series (*co-published with Terres et Vie*)

African Gardens and Orchards	ISBN 0-333-49076-2
Vanishing Land and Water	0-333-44597-X
Ways of Water	0-333-57078-2
Agriculture in African Rural Communities	0-333-44595-3

Contents

Acknowledgements

This book, as do most, owes much to many. I first became aware of this series when Rex Parry asked me to review, or to suggest reviewers for, some of the earlier manuscripts. It seemed reasonable to suggest that this volume would form a useful addition to the series. Animal agriculture has been divorced from crop agriculture for too long and any attempt to bring them together must be a step in the right direction.

At the beginning I had useful discussions with Sahr Lebbie and other colleagues in Ethiopia. Subsequently Oswin Perera and Mike Bryant contributed to the book's development in Vienna. At this stage I also had the opportunity to learn something of South American systems in long sessions with, among others, Bessie Urquieta and Julio Sumar. A course I conducted for trainees from many parts of the world and further travel out of Austria broadened my knowledge of systems in North Africa, the Near East and Asia.

In transferring from Austria to The Gambia I met Simon Chater in The Hague: he took up where Rex Parry left off and was responsible for helping get the book through the later development stages. In The Gambia, and in travels in West Africa associated with my stay there, I benefited from discussions with people from throughout the West African humid zones: in particular I thank Bill Snow for allowing me to use material from his excellent analysis of the tsetse and trypanosomiasis situation in West Africa.

Mary says that, thanks (each in its own way) to the personal computer and her garden, she has been less associated with this book than with earlier ones. That is only partly true: frequent cold and late meals and her advice and support throughout testify to her continuing and unstinting contribution. Andrew has again helped in his own inimitable way.

All photographs are by the author.

Preface

This is the tenth in a series of fifteen books on animal production in the tropics (the ones already published are on poultry, sheep, pigs, rabbits, ruminant nutrition, dairying, animal breeding, animal health and goats). The series is intended to provide up-to-date information for students, extension specialists and farmers, written in an accessible manner. All the books are produced by specialists who have worked in a number of tropical countries or regions. This volume is written by Trevor Wilson, who has considerable experience of livestock production in many parts of the tropics, having spent much of his professional life working for international organisations specialising in agriculture in developing countries.

Other books in the series have dealt either with the husbandry of individual species or with specific disciplines. This book shows how individual species of domestic livestock are or can be integrated within the agricultural system as a whole in the tropics. To put the subject in context the author starts with an overview of the domestication of the animals and the impact that domestic animals have had on human development.

The main part of the book is devoted to a series of case studies covering most, if not all, of the systems of livestock husbandry used in the tropics. The reasons that these systems have developed are outlined, their limitations highlighted and the ways in which they could be improved are discussed. This part of the book is a highly useful short reference work presenting the main features of the extremely varied livestock production systems found across the tropics.

Readers of this book will obtain a good insight into how livestock and crop husbandry can be linked in the wetter regions of the tropics to improve the use of resources. In the drier regions of the tropics crop husbandry is not an option, and so animal husbandry is the only way of using these regions for the benefit of people. The book explains why this is so and why these systems are now under threat.

By reading this book in conjunction with others in the series readers will understand why livestock are an important component of agriculture in the tropics, and how they are essential for the development of ecologically sound systems of food production.

Anthony J. Smith
Edinburgh, January 1995

PART 1
Background

1 Distribution and importance of livestock in the tropics

Distribution and numbers

Cattle

Since domestication, cattle have spread to all parts of the world and have been introduced wherever people have explored and settled. They are now by far the most numerous and, in overall terms, the most important of all the domestic herbivores. With the exception of the Hindu religion, there are few taboos against their full exploitation.

Because of this importance and their major roles as producers of milk, meat and power there are few habitats that, with human help, they have failed to conquer. The tsetse-infested areas of Africa are among these, in spite of resistance to trypanosomiasis in some types. Very highly productive dairy genotypes tend to perform poorly in humid tropical conditions unless management, nutritional and health conditions approach the ideal and unless climatic stress can be artificially reduced.

Cattle are more numerous in Asia than any other continent and about half of Asian cattle are found in India. There are also large numbers in the remainder of the Indian sub-continent, especially in Pakistan and Bangladesh. Over much of humid Asia, particularly the south-eastern part of the continent and in Indo-China, the buffalo largely replaces cattle. In spite of their very large numbers, cattle in Asia are at a relatively low density because of the vast area and there are also few cattle per person on account of the large human population.

Ethiopia is the African country with most cattle, closely followed by Nigeria. Cattle are outnumbered by buffalo in Egypt and they are replaced to a considerable extent by camels and both species of small ruminants in the arid areas surrounding the Sahara desert. Small numbers of more or less trypanotolerant *Bos taurus* are found in the humid and tsetse-infested areas of West and parts of Central Africa but much of the forested area of Central Africa is devoid of cattle. Cattle are intermediate

1

in density and in their ratio to the human population in Africa by comparison with Asia and South America, but some areas inhabited by Bantu tribes, such as Swaziland and other parts of southern Africa, have very high densities and high cattle to people ratios.

World cattle numbers increased by about 5 per cent during the 1980s. Africa's increase in this period was at about the world rate but in Asia the increase was in the region of 10 per cent.

Buffalo

The 'natural' range of the buffalo is the hot or warm humid zone of the Indian sub-continent and South and South-east Asia. They are most numerous in India, where more than half the world's buffalo are found. Buffalo are extremely important in a number of countries, where they might outnumber cattle, but their total world population of 122 million is equivalent to about 10 per cent of that of cattle.

Following India, China has the largest population of buffalo. Pakistan, Nepal and Bangladesh have large populations in the Indian sub-continent. In the Far East, Thailand, the Philippines, Indonesia, Vietnam and Burma each have buffalo populations in excess of 2 million. Egypt is the only African country with a large buffalo population of about 2.5 million.

In South America, where the buffalo has been introduced, Brazil has by far the largest numbers and there are other populations in Venezuela and Trinidad. In the Northern Territory of Australia buffalo have become feral and increased rapidly in numbers in the Kakadu area: elsewhere in Oceania there are a few buffalo in Papua New Guinea.

Wherever the buffalo is found it appears to be increasing in numbers. This is particularly the case where it has been recently introduced, for example in Brazil, and annual increments in numbers of 10 per cent are common. The feral Australian population has resulted from the introduction of only 83 animals, in three lots, between 1826 and 1843. Overall buffalo numbers increased by 1.1 per cent per year during the 1980s.

Goats

In the late 1980s the world population of goats was estimated at about 500 million, of which about 94 per cent were in tropical and sub-tropical areas. Some 40 per cent of tropical and 35 per cent of world goats are found in Africa. On this continent goats are concentrated in the arid and semi-arid regions of western Africa, the Sudan, the Horn of Africa and eastern Africa. Increases in the goat population of about 20 per cent overall are estimated to have taken place from 1974 to 1984 in these areas, where they are second to cattle in numbers. Goats are fewer but still a major element of the species mix in the drier areas of southern Africa. There are few goats, or indeed any domestic species, in west-central Africa, but small trypanotolerant types are quite common and more numerous than other species in the humid tsetse infested areas of coastal West Africa and its hinterland.

The Indian sub-continent is the next most important area for goats with about 30 per cent of the tropical population of the species. Here they are concentrated in the arid to semi-arid densely populated areas of the central highlands and in the mountainous regions of the north. The Near and Middle East also have large numbers of goats amounting to about 15 per cent of tropical numbers. Although there has been much recent interest in small ruminants (goats and sheep) in research and development circles in eastern Asia, in Central America and the Caribbean, and in South America, goats are found here in low numbers, at low densities and at low goat to human ratios, and represent only 4, 3 and 5 per cent, in the three areas, of the total tropical population. Goat numbers have increased by 12.0 per cent in the tropics in the last decade.

Sheep

Sheep are more numerous in the tropics than goats, with a total population of some 500 million. They are proportionally less important than goats, however, in world numbers, accounting for somewhat less than 45 per cent of all sheep. Africa has the largest population of tropical sheep, about 37 per cent of all sheep in the zone being found there. The areas of concentration are similar to those for goats. There are far fewer sheep proportionally in the Indian sub-continent than there are goats, and here they represent only 14 per cent of tropical numbers. In eastern Asia (1 per cent) and Central America and the Caribbean (2 per cent) sheep are of very minor importance.

In recent years sheep numbers have increased very slowly, by about 7 per cent in the tropics between 1978 and 1987. The increase has been above the average in Africa (10 per cent), less than the average in the Americas (3 per cent) and about the average in Asia (7 per cent). Sheep outnumber goats in the ratio 5:4 in tropical countries. With few exceptions goats are more important than sheep in humid areas (although paradoxically most goats are found in dry countries) in all the major tropical areas.

Camels

The normal distributional range of the one-humped camel (dromedary) is the African and Asian tropical and sub-tropical dry areas. With few exceptions camels are found in areas where rainfall is low and occurs in a relatively short period followed by a long hot dry season of eight or more months. These are the prevailing conditions in the deserts of northern Africa and over western Asia and the Indian sub-continent. The northern and western edges of the dromedary's range in Africa are the Mediterranean sea and the Atlantic ocean. The southern limit is also generally related to climate but historic and human factors play a role on this boundary. In Africa, the southern limit can be found at about 15 °N in West Africa from the Senegal coast through central Mali and the south of Niger. In Chad and the Sudan the southern limit has been put at 13 °N although in recent years the normal range has gradually been pushed southward. A biotic factor limiting the distribution of the camel in the south is the presence of tsetse and other biting flies.

In eastern Africa the arid conditions on the Red Sea coast, in the Gulf of Aden and in the hinterland of the Indian Ocean coast as far south as 2 °S are favourable to the camel. In Asia dromedaries extend northwards into Turkey, southern Russia and Afghanistan.

Essentially a wide-ranging species, the camel is the domestic animal of nomads. The nomadic owners of the dromedary are obliged to take their camels with them to assure their basic needs of transport, meat and milk. In eastern Africa the gradual spread of the camel to tribes not owning it in ancient times has resulted from a pre-existing nomadic or semi-nomadic way of life. The greatest cultural impact on the recent distribution of the camel has been Islam. As Arabs spread their faith they took the camel with them, consolidating its range northwards and eastwards in Asia and westwards along the Mediterranean littoral.

Until the arrival of motorised transport and the monetarisation of desert economies, the camel remained almost the only burden and personal transport animal in the areas to which it was adapted. Although these developments have considerably affected the transport role of the camel they have had much less effect on its cultural importance.

There were an estimated 18.5 million camels in the world in 1988. Of these, probably 16.5 million were one-humped camels in the tropics. More than 80 per cent of all Arabian camels are found in Africa, and East Africa contains about 63 per cent of all Old World Camelidae. Somalia and Sudan account for 70 per cent of camels in Africa, while Ethiopia, Chad and Kenya contain a further 12 per cent. Apart from these countries, Mauritania, Niger and Mali have important populations, as do the Maghreb countries of Algeria, Morocco and Tunisia. In Asia, about 70 per cent of dromedaries are found in the Indian sub-continent.

There has been a steady increase in camel numbers over the past decade. Where numbers have decreased they have done so for two unrelated reasons. In countries in which oil is now the principal commodity, the nomadic way of life is no longer the major one, and there has been a steady decrease in the number of camels over recent years. The second reason for reduction in numbers is the severe drought conditions of the 1970s and 1980s, although losses of camels compared with other classes of domestic stock have been minimal.

Pigs

The pig is subject to many taboos which have affected its distribution and numbers. It is thus virtually absent from large areas of the Middle East and North Africa where Islam is the dominant religion. It is also uncommon in Ethiopia, where Orthodox Christianity in the highlands maintains the Old Testament prohibition against eating pig meat and where the lowland populations are mainly Moslem.

The pig's omnivorous habits have been capitalised on to a greater extent in Asia and also in Oceania. In some of the Pacific Islands the pig is the most important of all domestic quadrupeds and found at high density and at a high ratio in relation to people.

Africa has relatively few pigs in relation to other tropical areas and also in relation to the domestic herbivore species. The main reasons for this are undoubtedly cultural and religious but are also related to ecology over much of the continent. In the vast areas of forest which characterise humid Africa the pig is usually a much more important component of the range of domestic species, especially in view of the absence of cattle.

World pig numbers increased by 8 per cent in the 10-year period from 1980. There was a 20 per cent increase in Africa, a 3 per cent increase in South America and a 12 per cent increase in Asia.

Equidae

With few exceptions the current distribution of equines reflects the centres of origin and the physiological adaptations of horses and donkeys. Horses are, therefore, usually more numerous in the cooler and moister tropical areas or at higher altitudes. Donkeys are commonest in the harsher semi-arid and arid areas. African Horse Sickness limits distribution and numbers of horses in many tropical areas. Cultural and historical factors also affect the distribution of equines, especially mules.

In world terms it is Asia that has most horses, mules and donkeys but by far the largest number of these are in China. Donkeys and mules are almost wholly absent from the whole of humid South-east Asia and from Indo-China: in some countries in these sub-regions horses are not uncommon and occur at relatively high densities but at a low ratio to the human population. In the Indian sub-continent, Bangladesh has very few donkeys while both India and Pakistan (which has the third largest number of donkeys of all countries in the world) have large numbers at relatively high densities but again at a low ratio to humans.

Donkeys are far more common in Africa than horses and, with the exception of Ethiopia in the tropical areas, there are very few mules. Ethiopia, has, in fact about 65 per cent of all African mules, almost 50 per cent of horses and 30 per cent of donkeys. There are also many donkeys in Egypt but few horses. Mali, Niger and Sudan provide examples of the dominance of donkeys over horses in hot, dry areas.

There was a small annual increase in the world horse population of less than 0.3 per cent in the decade of the 1980s. The horse population actually decreased very slightly in Africa in this period, as in Asia, but there was an overall increase of 16 per cent in South America.

Poultry

Throughout history both domestic fowl and the common duck have maintained their popularity in their areas of domestication in the humid tropical areas of South-east Asia. Fowl, however, have also become popular almost everywhere in the world while ducks, except for some very special exceptions in developed economies, are still largely confined to Asia. The other species of poultry are of minor importance in the tropics, with turkeys, for example, representing less than 9 per cent of the world population. Asia has almost 40 per cent of world poultry and 85 per cent of ducks.

Poultry are less important in Africa than elsewhere in the tropics. Particularly in the dry areas, which might coincidentally have large ruminant populations, they are of minor importance. The major exception is Burkina Faso, which has by far the highest density of fowl and the highest ratio of fowl to humans on the continent.

The potential for rapid expansion inherent in poultry populations and their suitability for providing small quantities of animal protein at low cost appear to have been fully exploited in the last few years. World numbers of domestic fowl increased by 35 per cent in the 1980s, of ducks by more than 20 per cent and of turkeys by almost 25 per cent. These simple figures, moreover, do not reflect the genetic improvements that have been achieved in the same time, which have resulted in increased egg production and much more efficient use of feed for both eggs and meat.

Contrary to trends in almost all other aspects of agricultural production in Africa, where growth has lagged behind human population expansion, the increase in the poultry population appears to have kept pace with it, at an annual rate of about 3 per cent growth of the human population. In Asia a massive 7 per cent per annum increase in fowl numbers and a commendable 2 per cent annual increase in duck populations have been achieved since 1980.

Importance and production functions

Relative importance of domestic livestock

In numerical terms cattle are by far the most important quadruped livestock in the tropics. About 2 in every 5 domestic four-legged animals are cattle, 1 in 4 are sheep, 1 in 5 are goats, 1 in 15 are pigs and 1 in 18 are buffalo. Assessing the importance of the various species on a tropical or on a local scale is not, however, an easy task. Numbers alone are obviously inadequate. The weight of animals, expressed as a percentage of the weight of all animals, perhaps represents a slightly better approach as this measure takes account of differences in size and can also give some indication of the amount of resources used by a species. The Standard Stock Unit of 500 kg is sometimes used but this has little meaning over much of the tropics, where very few animals weigh that much. A measure often used is the Tropical Livestock Unit (TLU) of 250 kg, which more nearly represents the weight of a zebu cow or the average weight of a single bovine in a herd of mixed age and sex. Species other than cattle are usually expressed as a fraction or multiple of a TLU with sheep, for example, often being calculated as 0.1 TLU.

An even more appropriate measure of importance is the calculated average weight of all animals in a single species herd. This figure, the Mean Population Weight (MPW), is calculated on representative groups of animals in sex and age cohorts within different types of herds or flocks and for different species. This measure also indicates the proportion of feed resources likely to be used by the different species of herbivores. Under such a system, cattle constitute about 72 per cent of all domestic herbivores (Table 1.1) and are very important in South America where the population of almost 1 million buffalo in Brazil becomes relatively very insignificant. Cattle are of lesser importance in Asia, where there are large numbers of buffalo, and in Oceania, where sheep contribute greatly to the Domestic Herbivore Biomass (DHB).

Pigs and poultry do not fall easily into the foregoing classification, mainly on account of their different feed preferences. The importance of these two classes of animal might best be measured in terms of their relative proportion to total herbivore biomass. Biomass alone, however, is also a rather unsatisfactory measure of the importance of domestic animals. It does not, for example, provide any measure of milk production (70 per cent of milk drunk by people in India is from buffaloes) or of the value of work. Nor does it take account of reproductive and survival rates, which in turn influence the contribution of animals to the well-being of people, in particular in products which can be eaten or sold and which are generally known as offtake.

Table 1.1 Relative importance of animals in terms of domestic herbivore biomass and of non-herbivores in relation to herbivores

Area/Country	Per cent of DHB[1]					Relative importance[2]	
	Cattle	Buffalo	Goats and Sheep	Camelids	Equines	Pigs	Domestic fowl
World	72	10	9	1	8	3.84	0.341
Africa	74	1	9	9	7	5.36	1.258
Benin	80	0	20	0	<1	5.29	0.142
Botswana	90	0	3	0	7	470.89	4.238
Cameroon	47	0	52	0	1	7.84	0.856
Chad	75	0	8	11	6	963.25	2.890
Côte d'Ivoire	76	0	24	0	0	8.81	0.248
Egypt	20	32	28	1	19	612.67	0.306
Ethiopia	71	0	10	3	16	413.42	2.619
Gabon	38	0	62	0	0	1.00	0.077
Kenya	76	0	13	7	4[3]	26.28	1.195
Madagascar	85	0	14	0	1	9.12	0.621
Niger	58	0	19	9	14	416.63	1.055
Nigeria	71	0	23	<1	6	31.67	0.235
Somalia	34	0	19	47	14	4 189.90	13.966
Sudan	73	0	12	13	2	–	1.787
Zaire	79	0	21	0	0	6.54	0.273
South America	88	<1	4	<1	7	3.96	0.515
Bolivia	67	0	15	6	12	12.41	0.026
Brazil	90	<1	2	0	7	5.34	0.328
Colombia	87	0	1	0	12	12.25	0.854
Ecuador	82	0	5	<1	13	1.63	0.162
Peru	52	0	21	8	19	10.88	0.554

Table 1.1 (*cont'd*)

| Area/Country | Per cent of DHB[1] | | | | | Relative importance[2] | |
	Cattle	Buffalo	Goats and Sheep	Camelids	Equines	Pigs	Domestic fowl
Asia							
Bangladesh	59	24	9	<1	7	3.71	0.314
India	88	8	4	0	<1	–	0.542
Indonesia	65	29	5	<1	<1	49.74	2.501
Laos	52	28	14	0	6	4.56	0.071
Pakistan	31	66	<1	0	2	1.13	0.220
Philippines	38	37	13	3	8	–	0.067
Sri Lanka	30	61	4	0	5	0.99	0.138
Syria	59	39	2	0	<1	34.49	0.372
Yemen	31	0	57	<1	11	14 689.00	?
Oceania	42	0	25	7	26	–	0.424
Fiji	58	0	41	0	1	50.83	3.711
New Caledonia	77	0	3	0	20	8.93	0.130
Papua New Guinea	91	0	2	0	.7	3.53	0.152
Tonga	98	0	2	0	<1	0.09	0.048
Vanuatu	44	0	6	0	50	0.43	?
	98	0	1	0	1	1.59	?

Notes:

1 DHB = domestic herbivore biomass at assumed mean population weights of: cattle 210 kg, buffalo 250 kg, goats 18 kg, sheep 30 kg, one-humped camels 300 kg, South American camelids 40 kg, equines 250 kg

2 Ratio of species to all herbivores

3 Includes horses only for equines as, although donkeys are present, they are not enumerated

Source: adapted from FAO. 1988. *Production yearbook, Volume 42.* Food and Agriculture Organisation: Rome, Italy

Table 1.2 Production functions of domestic animals in the service of people

Major category	Actual contribution	Livestock species
Meat	Fresh, dried, salted	All (but minor in equines)
Milk	Fresh, dried, fermented, skimmed	All ruminants
	Butter, cheese, ghee, buttermilk, whey	All ruminants
Eggs	Fresh, dried	All poultry
Fibres	Wool	Sheep, alpaca
	Hair	Goat, camel, sheep
	Silk	Silk worm
Skins	Hides	Large ruminants, camel
	Skins	Small ruminants, pig, ostrich
	Pelts and fur	Sheep, rabbit, minor species
	Containers	Ruminants
Feathers	Fashion	Ostrich, peafowl, domestic fowl
	Down	Duck, goose
	Quill pens	Goose
Power	Ploughing, weeding and other field operations	Equines, cattle, buffalo, camel
	Transport (cart, pack, riding)	Equines, cattle, buffalo, camel, alpaca
	Agricultural support (water lifting, threshing, etc.)	Equines, cattle, buffalo, camel
Faeces/urine	Fertiliser	All
	Fuel (direct, methane)	All
	Building material	All
	Livestock feed	Poultry (minor for other species)
Culture, sport, recreation	Companionship	All (but especially minor species)
	Exhibitions, shows	All
	Racing	Horse, camel, buffalo
	Riding, hunting	Horse, camel
	Sacrifice	All (except equines)
	Dowry, blood money	Ruminants, camel
	Fighting	Cattle, buffalo, fowl, camel, sheep
Pest control	Weeds in crops	All
	Weeds in irrigation	Buffalo, duck, goose
	Snails	Buffalo, duck, goose
	Insects	Poultry
Others	Security	All
	Capital accumulation	All
	Honey	Bees
	Cosmetic raw materials	Ruminants
	Fertiliser and feed (hoofs, horns, bones, condemned meat)	All

More than meat and milk

At national level, meat and milk production dominate research and development thinking and planning for the livestock sector. However, animals provide far more products and fulfil many more functions than these obvious items (Table 1.2).

More than 85 per cent of tropical livestock are owned by smallholder mixed farmers or by other traditional groups. The priorities of these people, in respect of livestock, are the reverse of a list that would be established by most politicians, scientists or commercial farmers. In order, it is probable that the priorities of small scale and traditional livestock owners in the tropics are:

- reducing and spreading risk;
- generating and accumulating capital;
- providing services in support of crop production (power, fertiliser and, in some areas, fuel);
- fulfilling social, cultural and religious requirements and obligations;
- providing status or prestige within the immediate community;
- providing food and other direct products; and
- generating income.

It is true that, as in specialised operations, most livestock finally fulfil either or both of the last two listed functions. It is equally true that the perceived priorities of farmers in the tropics mean that they pay little attention to improving the food-producing function of animals or to achieving high cash returns. These are the principal reasons why it has seldom been easy to transfer supposedly improved technology or livestock breeds directly to tropical agricultural systems.

Animals contribute to human welfare in many ways. In the tropics a major role is their complementarity to crops. They contribute to improved agriculture, mainly through the provision of power and by the supply of manure. In turn they benefit from agriculture by their use of forages and crop residues and by-products as sources of feed. In a mix of different animal species they also contribute to long-term sustainability by the complementary use of different feed resources (Table 1.3) or of similar feed resources at different heights above the ground (Fig 1.1). Not least important are their functions as a human food buffer in times of crop shortage and as a temporary and longer term store of wealth. The various lengths of animals' life cycles, production at different times of the year and the multiplicity of products they supply are important facets of these functions.

Table 1.3 Feeding patterns of three domestic livestock species in an agro-pastoral system in central Mali

Feed resource	Species (per cent of time on resource)		
	Goat	Sheep	Cattle
Field layer	11	59	53
Browse cover	87	34	4
Crop by-products and stubbles			
Millet	2	7	6
Rice	0	0	37
Total annual feeding time (hours)	2061	1948	2883

Source: Wilson, R.T., de Leeuw, P.N. and de Haan, C. 1983. *Recherches sur less systèmes en zones arides: Resultats préliminaires (Rapport de recherche N° 5)*. International Livestock Centre for Africa: Addis Ababa, Ethiopia

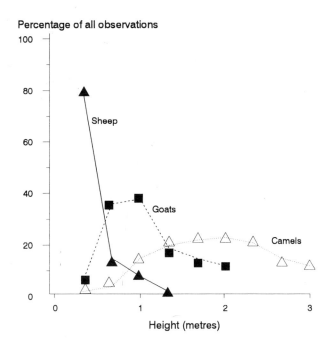

Fig 1.1 *Comparative times spent feeding at different heights by camels, goats and sheep in northern Kenya (Source: Schwartz, H.J. 1983. Improved utilization of arid rangelands through multiple species herds.* Proc. 5th World Conf. Anim. Prod. *2: pp. 625–626)*

2 Classifying, describing and improving production systems

Classifications

There are many possible classifications of production systems which include livestock.

In Africa a common classification uses the degree of movement as a descriptor:

- nomadic systems – irregular movement in search of feed and water and no fixed base;
- transhumant systems – regular seasonal movement with returns to a fixed base for at least part of the year; and
- sedentary systems – where animal movement is restricted to a very short radius from a permanent fixed base.

In its strict sense transhumance has a rather rigid definition of vertical movement from lowland areas, where animals are kept in the winter, to the Alpine pastures of the summer season. In the tropics, however, the term tends to be used more broadly.

Other classifications might include:

- geographical considerations (both physical and political);
- climatic type;
- the land use intensity;
- the type of crop or animal; or
- the production objectives (such as meat, milk, fibre or draught).

A systems definition combining many of these features (Table 2.1) might also include considerations of sustainability and other objectives of production, such as the market for the farm's output.

Whether a system is 'modern' or 'traditional' is another variable that can be taken into account in identifying the major categories of system. Here the principal factors taken into consideration would comprise many of those used in other classifications. The principal sources of feed could be included, as also could the main factors of

Table 2.1   A possible classification of production systems involving livestock

System type	Livestock species	Crop species	Primary production target	Risks	Sustainability
Intensive specialised	Dairy cattle; pigs; poultry; rabbits	Coffee; tea; cocoa; rubber; fibres	Urban or export markets	High biological (including species-specific diseases) and economic (dependence on world prices)	Doubtful unless high levels of recycling can be assured
Intensive diversified	Dairy cattle; pigs; poultry; rabbits	Coffee; tea; cocoa; rubber; fibres; vegetables	Urban or export markets	Less than intensive specialised as not dependent on single animal or crop	Better than intensive specialised as crop and animal residues can complement each other
Combined on/off farm	Multiple	Multiple	Urban, peri-urban and rural markets; farm consumption	Low as multiple species of crops and livestock complement each other; off-farm income can be invested in farm enterprises	Good, especially if off-farm activities are integrated with those on farm and located near to it
Extensive farming and livestock	Many, including camels and small ruminants	Many, including coarse grains	Mainly home consumption and local markets	High to low, depending on ecosystem (arid to sub-humid) but helped by system diversity	Can be high if livestock and crops are well integrated and farming activities do not extend too far into arid areas
Subsistence	Multiple	Multiple	Almost entirely home use with occasional surpluses for	High to low, worse in high population density and intensive land use zones in marginal areas	Variable but decreasing in many areas due to expanding human populations

Table 2.2 Traditional and modern livestock production systems

Type	System	Macro-management	Main production factors	Nutrient source
Traditional	Pastoral	Nomadic/Semi-sedentary	Land	Range
	Agro-pastoral	Transhumant/Sedentary	Land/Labour	Range/Crop by-products
	Agricultural	Sedentary	Labour/Land	Crop by-products/Household waste
	Urban	Sedentary	Labour	Household waste/Feed
Modern	Ranching	Sedentary	Land/Capital	Range/Forage
	Feedlot	Sedentary	Capital/Labour	Feed/Forage
	Dairy farm	Sedentary	Capital/Labour/Land	Feed/Forage
	Research station	Sedentary	Land/Labour/Capital	Range/Forage/Feed

Source: adapted from Wilson, R.T. 1988. Small ruminant production systems in tropical Africa. *Small Rumin. Res.* 1: pp. 305–25.

Table 2.3 Some major crop-animal systems in the tropics

System	Animal species	Crops	Feed sources[1]	Animal importance	Regions
Fishing and farming complex	Pigs Ducks Cattle, goats	Coconut, cassava, rice, cocoa	By-products Fish waste, rice bran Pasture under coconuts	Medium	East and South-east Asia; Coastal East Africa
Market gardens	Pigs Ducks Fish	Intensive vegetables	By-products, purchased feed	High	Lowland East and South-east Asia; Humid West Africa
Vegetables and mixed crops	Buffalo, cattle, sheep, goats Pigs	Vegetables, rice, sugar cane, sweet and Irish potatoes	By-products, cane tops, cut forage By-products, waste vegetables	High	Highland East and South-east Asia; Humid West Africa; Humid South America
Annual food crops	Buffalo, cattle, sheep, goats, pigs, poultry, equines	Maize, sorghum, millet, wheat, oilseeds, groundnut, cassava	By-products, range grasses, browse	High	Semi-arid Tropics
Shifting cultivation	Cattle, goats, sheep, poultry, pigs	Cereals, oilseeds, groundnut, vegetables, roots and tubers	By-products, range grasses, browse	High to medium	Semi-arid to Humid Tropics
Annual and perennial cash crops	Cattle, goats, sheep, poultry, pigs	Coffee, cocoa, tea, sisal, banana, pineapple	By-products, waste, purchased feed	Medium to high	Sub-humid to Humid Tropics
Orchard and tree crops	Cattle, goats, sheep, poultry, pigs	Coconut, oil palm, cashew, citrus, rubber, cocoa	By-products, waste, under-storey grazing, fallow	Medium to low	Lowland Sub-humid to Humid Tropics

Table 2.3 (*cont'd*)

System	Animal species	Crops	Feed sources[1]	Animal importance	Regions
Irrigated agriculture	Buffalo, cattle, sheep, goats, poultry, fish, pigs	Rice, sugar, vegetables	By-products, molasses, waste vegetables	High to low	Tropics
Highland mixed farming	Cattle, goats, sheep, poultry, equines	Wheat, barley, maize, sorghum, millet, pulses, legumes	By-products, range grazing, browse, fallow	High to medium	Tropics > 1500 m altitude
Urban	Cattle, goats, sheep, poultry, pigs	Vegetables on small scale	Vegetable/household waste, purchased fodder, compounds	High	Tropics
Traditional pastoral	Camels, cattle, goats, sheep, poultry, equines	Dates/vegetables in oases, short-cycle vegetables	Range grazing, browse	Very high	Arid to Semi-arid Tropics
Commercial ranching	Cattle, sheep, rarely goats	Of little importance, some forage and cereals	Range grazing, forage	Very high	Arid to Semi-arid Tropics
Commercial dairying	Cattle, goats, sheep	Varying importance, grains and forage	Range and improved grazing, forage, purchased feed	Very high	Tropics

Note:

1 By-products include crop residues and stubbles, by-products from home processing and agro-industrial by-products

Source: Adapted from McDowell, R.E. and Hilderbrand, P.E. 1980. *Integrated crop and animal production: Making the most of resources available to small farms in developing countries.* The Rockefeller Foundation: Washington DC, USA

production (land, labour and capital) used in economic analyses (Table 2.2).

For the purposes of this book, farming systems will be considered in the major context of crop/livestock interactions. This classification takes into consideration dominant crops, the major species of domestic animals and the main feed resources and feed types utilised by the animal component of the system (Table 2.3).

The most important types of system comprise major, and possibly minor, species of livestock, one or a limited number of major crops, and minor crops ranging from none to numerous. Where crops are important in the system they often determine the major feed source, in which case they may also exert a considerable influence on the type of animal kept. The flow of nutrients through a system is important for that system's viability and efficiency. Making better uses of nutrients normally not eaten or otherwise converted to production by humans is an important advantage of keeping animals in many parts of the tropics.

Farming systems research

Systems are normally described in pluridisciplinary studies. These studies usually cover not only the cropping or farming system but also the whole environment in which the production takes place. This environment includes political, economic and social factors as well as ecological ones. Such an approach is generally known as farming systems research (Fig 2.1). This research passes through several stages, often referred to as description, diagnosis, design, experimentation, and evaluation.

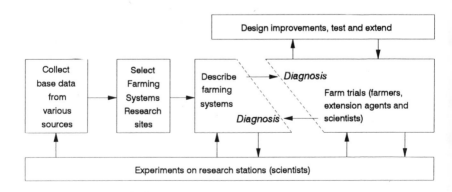

Fig 2.1 *A diagrammatic representation of farming systems research*

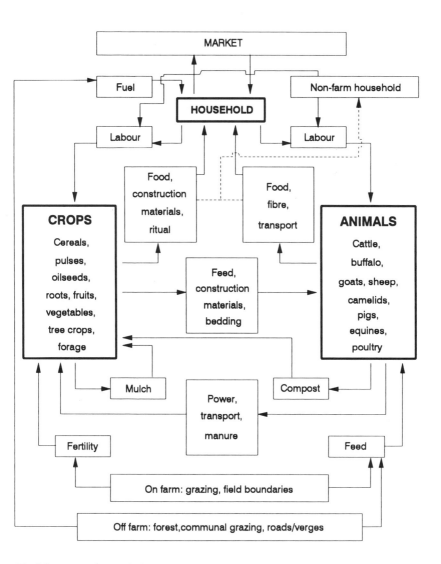

Fig 2.2 *A simple model of animal-crop interactions and dynamics in a mixed farming system in the tropics*

Properly planned and executed farming systems research will lead, in the early stages, to a clear understanding of the dynamics of a system (Fig 2.2) and in the later stages to raising agricultural output and human living standards. As research proceeds there should be feedback from one stage to the previous ones, and the whole process tends to a cyclic nature. The fact that much farming systems research fails, even at the description and diagnosis stages, will be evident from some of the case studies presented in the following chapters. Unfortunately, many systems studies have been 'multi' rather than 'inter' disciplinary; some remained at the diagnostic phase, failing to move into design and testing; still other studies have tended to introduce a package of innovations too radical or expensive for most farmers to wish to risk. An important but often neglected aspect of mixed systems is how they affect the use and efficiency of labour. Innovations that demand too much additional work are seldom adopted.

It has often been considered that modern systems are dynamic, productive and responsive to innovations and change, while traditional systems are static, unproductive and conservative. Both views are stereotypic. There are 'conservative' farmers in modern systems and 'progressive' farmers in traditional ones. Advances in productivity in both types of system are likely to be achieved only where new technology:

- is fitted to the prevailing conditions;
- does not increase the risk of instability;
- does not create too much additional work, and
- produces sufficiently attractive biological and economic returns.

More recently, it has been taken into account that innovations should not lead to the degradation of natural resources and that they should be sustainable in the long term.

Summary

There are biotic, abiotic and social factors which influence the components of an agricultural system and the relative importance of those components. Animals need to be selected in combinations of species and numbers to match the feed resources available. Crops have to be chosen to match climate and soils as well as the availability of labour, and to take account of human food preferences and market opportunities.

The animal-crop interface concentrates nutrients, recycled through animal dung, on to the arable areas and animals supply power for crop operations. In return the cropped areas provide energy and protein feeds for the animals, sometimes in large quantities and at times of the production cycle when other feeds may be in low supply and of poor quality. A diversity of animal and crop enterprises within a system, possibly allied to some sale of labour for wages, contributes to both biological and economic stability. Animals in mixed systems contribute long-term stability to both traditional and modern systems and help to sustain production over otherwise difficult periods.

PART 2

3 The swidden system in Asia

The swidden, or slash-and-burn system, covers about 30–40 per cent of all tropical Asia. Average farm size is about 2 ha, all of which is cultivated by hand using a hoe and a dibbing stick. Plant residues are normally left in the field to provide mulch. The main livestock are chickens and pigs but there are also goats and sheep. Little 'management' is practised as the animals are left to scavenge. Thus, there is no systematic recycling of plant nutrients but some manure may be gathered and used on crops near the home. The farmed areas are intercropped to numerous crops, mostly annuals, but there are a few perennial ones. The land is usually fallowed after 2–4 years of cropping. Human population densities are low, household fuel is no problem and there is little integration of animals and crops.

There is little farm infrastructure and few capital inputs or services are available from outside the immediate family or village. Within the village, however, there is considerable co-operation. Animals are not reared for any specific purpose or for sale but are sold to meet short-term emergency needs or slaughtered to celebrate cultural or religious occasions. The dominant soil types are of poor quality and subject to erosion. Wild animals from the forest or the fallow areas may cause considerable damage to crops and some predators may take livestock.

Conclusions

The advantages of the system include:

- the low population pressure, allowing long-term fallows;
- the diversified cropping pattern, which can be used to advantage in soil conservation; and
- the lack of labour which prevents rapid expansion of the cropped area and thus further reduces the risks of erosion.

Disadvantages are:

- the poor access to markets; and
- scarcity of animals for draught and transport.

Modern developments, including ranching and logging, threaten the system by reducing the area available for agriculture, leading to a shortened fallow period in many areas.

Case study: Northern Thailand

Thailand provides a good example of livestock and crops in swidden farming. The populations of domestic ruminants in Thailand generally increased in the period 1975 to 1984: buffalo from 5.6 to 6.3 million; cattle from 4.1 to 4.8 million; goats from 48 000 to 74 000; and sheep are the exception, showing a decrease from 71 000 to 45 000. Approximately 70 per cent of northern Thailand is mixed deciduous forest with some major and world-renowned hardwood species, especially teak (*Tectona grandis*) and oak (*Quercus brandisiana*) and important softwoods including *Pinus* spp. The remaining 30 per cent is swidden, which has a mainly shrub and grass cover including bamboo and a grass, *Imperata cylindrica*, which is often considered a noxious weed. Animals are usually allowed free access to the grazing areas but may also be herded. They graze and browse the year round.

Estimated dry matter yield of forage available to animals in one study was 2400 kg/ha with a crude protein content of 8.3 per cent: dry matter yields of unimproved rubber and coconut plantations (i.e. those in which no effort was made to plant or encourage forage species) was 500 kg/ha and 1200 kg/ha with protein contents of about 14–16 per cent and 8–12 per cent respectively. Feed availability in the dry season gave problems, as did lack of water. No serious disease outbreaks were evident in animals, perhaps because of the low stocking rate, but sucking lice, blood-feeding flies and a nasal leech caused some problems. Even when animals were herded, roaming domestic dogs caused some losses, as herders were often occupied collecting wild products such as fuel, bamboo shoots and honey.

Conclusions

The major constraint identified in the system was the lack of dry-season forage during the hot period from February to mid-May. It was considered that the animal component, particularly goats, might have some negative impact on fallow regeneration, but livestock fed mainly on the understorey plants of little economic value as timber. Proper control of stocking rates could reduce any potential problems. In addition, some practices unconnected with livestock, such as burning to improve visibility or to encourage the growth of mushrooms, had more deleterious effects than did animal use.

The prospects for improving the system appear good. Returns from crops could be improved, and environmental stability enhanced, through the use of perennial crops, bunded paddies, terraces and reserved grazing areas in the swidden lands. These changes would allow large ruminants to assume a more important function in the system and assist in capital formation. A necessary educational step would be a change in attitude by policy makers, many of whom currently see the swidden system as wasteful of resources, contributing little to national economies in that it does not generate large export earnings.

4 Irrigated agriculture

Controlled or flood-plain irrigation is characteristic of many tropical areas but is especially prevalent in much of Asia and humid West Africa. Most rice producing areas have at least 3 months in which rainfall exceeds 200 mm and a short dry season of less than 6, but often of only 2, months duration. The length of the dry season may be a major factor affecting feed availability, but in some areas this problem can be reduced by letting weeds regenerate or by allowing stock to feed on canal banks and in drainage areas.

Population densities are high for people and can be high for animals. Although rice is the major crop, particularly for subsistence, green vegetables and food legumes can be important subsidiary enterprises. The newer 'green revolution' varieties of rice require heavy doses of fertiliser, some of which is or could be replaced by animal manure. Rice bran and hulls are available as by-products for animal feed, bran having up to 15 per cent crude protein as well as fairly high levels of oil or fat. Integrating livestock more closely with cropping could lead to intensification of this currently extensive system.

In Asia the major species of domestic animal are Swamp type buffalo, cattle, pigs, chickens, ducks and geese. In West Africa the principal species are cattle, sheep and goats. Large ruminants are kept to provide draught power and feed mainly on crop residues. Pigs are fed mainly on rice residues and cut grass and sold to generate cash. Ducks and geese act as scavengers, gleaning spilt grains in the stubbles and feeding around the irrigation canals. In Asia the large ruminants may be confined since farms are small and fragmented, but in West Africa they are herded extensively. In both Asia and West Africa fuel for cooking is a problem because of the intensity of the cropping system.

Conclusions

Advantages of the irrigated system include the possibilities of multiple or mixed cropping leading to reduced dependence on a single crop. In addition, farmers have some experience in the care of animals and labour is available to look after them. The risk of crop failure is thus reduced, making it possible to accumulate capital.

The disadvantages of the system are that multiple cropping reduces the grasses and weeds available to livestock and the opportunity cost of labour may be so high that keeping livestock becomes unprofitable. Additional disadvantages with the new high-yielding rice varieties are that the straw is of poor feeding quality and may require treatment or supplementation if fed to animals, and that they require the use of the pesticides and herbicides that may be inimical to fish and duck production. Mechanisation, especially in Asia, may remove some by-products from the immediate vicinity of farms and lead to the development of commercial livestock farms which could capture large markets to the detriment of small farmers.

Case study: Bangladesh

One third of the total land area of Bangladesh is flooded every year. Rainfall varies from 1200 mm/year to 3400 mm/year and the average temperature in summer is 34 °C. Population density, among the world's highest, is about 620 people/km^2. The average stocking rate of cattle and buffalo is some 0.4 ha/head (250/km^2). The livestock sector contributes about 4 per cent to Gross Domestic Product. Some 12 per cent of rural households are landless, 40 per cent farm less than 0.4 ha and a further 22 per cent farm less than 1 ha. The number of animals per rural household is small, but they make a considerable contribution to household subsistence (Table 4.1). In the early 1980s, livestock produced annually 2.3 million horsepower of draught, 0.3 million t of meat, 1.0 t million of milk and 4.5 million hides and skins. Total annual meat consumption was 3.3 kg/person and milk consumption 10.8 kg/person.

Livestock feed derives mainly from crop residues. More than 77 per cent of the land area is cultivated with rice but rice straw contributes more than 90 per cent of the potential feed from crop residues. Rice

Table 4.1 Livestock numbers and meat and milk production in Bangladesh, 1981

Item	Cattle	Buffalo	Goats	Sheep	Poultry
Total numbers (million)	21.9	0.5	10.2	0.5	n.a.
Meat production ('000 t)	204.9	4.7	62.8	2.7	22.4
Milk production ('000 t)	696.4	15.9	274.8	5.5	0.0

Source: adapted from Saadullah, M. and Das, S.C. 1987. Integrated crop and small ruminant systems in Bangladesh. In: Devendra, C. (ed), *Small ruminant production systems in South and South-east Asia.* International Development Research Centre: Ottawa, Canada: pp. 203–222

straw and other by-products are estimated to be capable of producing 2 kg of dry matter and 80 g of concentrate per animal per day. Other feed is available from canal banks, weeds and browse, but it is obvious that the shortage of feed is a severe restriction on livestock output at present stocking levels.

Goats constitute about 31 per cent of livestock numbers. Their feed requirements, however, are probably only about 4 per cent of the total animal need, and most of that is from sources not greatly used by other species. The proportions of 20 per cent of total meat and 28 per cent of total milk produced by goats are important indicators of their direct support to the human population, but these contributions should be considered in relation to the indirect support in the form of power provided by cattle and buffalo. Goats are particularly important for landless and very small farmers (with less than 0.4 ha), contributing 40 per cent of all animal numbers for these groups compared to 15 per cent or less for larger holdings.

Conclusions

A greater contribution from livestock to the national economy could be achieved by increasing the feed supply. Paradoxically, the intensification of the cropping system has reduced the amount of animal feed, not only because the new high-yielding rice varieties have short straw but because much of the crop now ripens during the monsoon and the straw rots in the field. Treatment methods that allow wet straw to be conserved, the replacement of straw that is currently used for fuel and building by other materials and the use of non-conventional agro-industrial by-products will increase feed availability. Non-conventional green roughages and other feeds, such as water hyacinths, could also increase the feed supply. The use of animal dung as a fertiliser, along with other organic materials, could lead to closer integration of livestock into the whole system, as could their use for biogas production.

Other possibilities for increased livestock production are improved management, the control of disease and selection and crossing of local genotypes.

Case study: Bogor district, West Java, Indonesia

In a 180 ha village at 350–450 m above sea level, cultivated land accounts for 50 per cent of the total area, 70 per cent of this being fully irrigated on terraces, 20 per cent semi-irrigated and 10 per cent is rainfed cropping. Of the non-cultivated land, 80 per cent is houses and compounds and 20 per cent roads. Annual rainfall is about 3770 mm with 8 months of the year having more than 200 mm rain

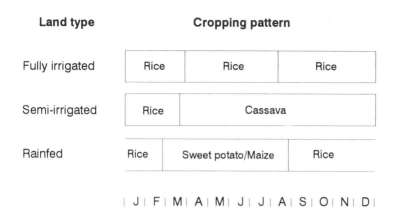

Land type	Cropping pattern		
Fully irrigated	Rice	Rice	Rice
Semi-irrigated	Rice	Cassava	
Rainfed	Rice	Sweet potato/Maize	Rice

| J | F | M | A | M | J | J | A | S | O | N | D |

Fig 4.1   *Cropping patterns in Bogor, West Java, Indonesia (Source: adapted from Petheram, R.J. 1986.* A farming systems approach to ruminant research in Java (Ph.D. Thesis). *University of New England: Armidale, Australia)*

and only 0–2 months having less than 100 mm. Temperature is in the range 15–30 °C and does not limit crop growth. Soils are deep, red-yellow sandy clays and are free-draining but puddle well for rice cultivation. Over 95 per cent of the population is Muslim. Because of the proximity of Bogor there are opportunities for wage labour but land is also being purchased in the village by town dwellers. More than half the village families own no land and average holding size for all owning families is less than 0.5 ha. Land sharing arrangements allow the landless to have access to this production factor, a common arrangement being one in which the owner provides all inputs except labour and the 'tenant' takes 20 per cent of the harvest. Grazing on roads, canal banks and other uncultivated areas is communal, crop residues can usually be had by simply asking and rice bran can be purchased from the village mill.

Cropping patterns vary not only with type of land (Fig 4.1) but with profitability, ease of marketing, capital and labour availability, recent rainfall, and water available for rice. The 60 per cent of households with a compound (average area 700 m²) plant banana, pawpaw, taro, cloves, nutmeg, jackfruit, coffee and many other tropical fruits. Hedges and trees on canal banks along roadsides provide browse and forage from *Gliricidia maculata, Leucaena leucocephala, Albizia falcataria* and *Maesopsis africana*, the last two also providing useful timber. In one year the village might produce 280 t of rice, 250 t of cassava, 150 t of sweet potato, 30 t of maize, 30 t of vegetables, 30 t of clove, 15 t of groundnut and some fruit from a resident population of about 4200 people.

27

Table 4.2   Livestock ownership in a village of predominantly irrigated rice in Bogor, West Java, Indonesia

Class of stock	Total number	Families rearing (% of 800)	Median flock size	Animal density (no./km²)
Domestic fowl	12 700	84	10	9 700
Sheep	1 000	30	5	540
Ducks	990	7	3	535
Goats	115	3	4	60
Buffalo	53	2	2	30
Rabbits	290	?	?	160

Source: adapted from Petheram, R.J. 1986. *A farming systems approach to ruminant research in Java (Ph.D. Thesis)*. University of New England: Armidale, Australia

Almost all families own some livestock but these are mostly domestic fowl (Table 4.2), which are kept mainly for ceremonial purposes, as a capital reserve, as food, and for sale, in that order of priority. Sheep, goats and ducks are all kept primarily as a capital reserve, then for ceremonial purposes and for sale. Buffalo are kept primarily to hire out to provide income and rabbits are kept as pets. Over half the goats and sheep are owned on a share basis, flocks that are share-owned being larger (5.8 head) than those individually owned (3.7 head).

Poultry are kept in bamboo cages at night and scavenge freely during the day. Sheep and goats are housed in bamboo pens with thatch or tile roofs and raised slatted floors: buffalo pens are also of bamboo but at ground level. All ruminants are hand fed on cut forage. Livestock are sold direct or through agents who visit the village. All ruminants are supposed to be slaughtered at official abattoirs but many are butchered in the village or for ceremonies. The only livestock support services that exist are for commercial poultry.

The buffalo herd is 70 per cent adult females, which are worked for as much as 5 hours/day for 180–300 days/year, mostly for ploughing. Pregnant females are usually worked right up to parturition. It is estimated that the total of 96 livestock units produced 11 000 kg of weight increase per year from the 800 t of forage dry matter provided, with a conversion rate of 7:1. Cassava, sweet potato and maize residues are the main feed resources for small ruminants, diets having a crude protein content of 13 per cent in the rains and 10 per cent in the dry season. Green and dry rice straw provide 55–60 per cent of buffalo feed, but this assures a dietary crude protein content of only 10 per cent in the wet and 8 per cent in the dry seasons. Because of the variety of feed available and the way it is fed, the small ruminants are not directly in competition with buffalo for their nutritional requirements. Manure is carefully collected and used on the farm or sold for cash.

Conclusions

In this village, livestock are generally well integrated into the overall system, but it is very inefficient: farmers collected 260 kg of green feed to obtain 1 kg of weight gain from their animals. Justifications for improving the system through research and investment are that livestock are traditionally accepted by farmers, there is marked potential for improvement (four times increased output has been obtained in on-farm trials) and technical productivity can be increased without prejudice to the main socio-economic reason for keeping livestock, which is as a capital reserve.

Case study: Duck egg production in West Java

Several systems or sub-systems of egg production from ducks are described from West Java. These include fully herded, fully scavenging (i.e. free ranging but not herded) and fully yarded systems as well as combinations of the three. Fully herded systems are commonest, with ducks under the control of the owner or a paid herder. Often several flocks are herded in loose associations with paid herders but with one of the owners in overall control. This last is usually responsible for decisions about movement and for overseeing the sale of eggs.

Most herding systems involve a considerable degree of 'nomadism' away from a home base. Ducks are walked or moved by small truck from one area to another. As many as 20 moves per year are made, covering a total distance of 400 km. The minimum economic size of a herded flock is 80 layers, with 120 birds the maximum that can be handled by one person. Herders are paid cash for their services or receive a variable proportion of the egg output.

Egg production is responsive to herder ability and experience and varies from as little as 24 per cent to as much as 93 per cent (that is, eggs laid per hundred ducks per day). It is also subject to fluctuations during the course of a year (Fig 4.2), in particular in relation to the availability of shallow flooded rice or of recently harvested areas of stubble.

In herded systems integration with agriculture is very close. Ducks follow the harvest and are herded during the day, then returned to a temporary pen in the late afternoon to lay their eggs. The diet comprises 77.2 per cent rice, 17.4 per cent snails (of five species) and smaller amounts of insects, frogs and grass. Intensification of yarding of ducks, which is common in smaller flocks, seems to depend on the availability

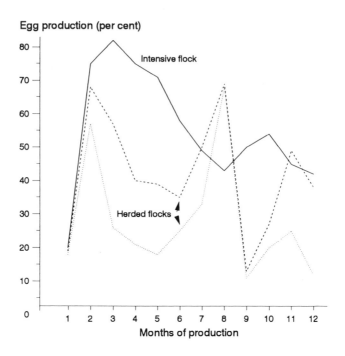

Fig 4.2 *Egg production by Tegal ducks in herded and intensive systems in West Java. (Source: Setioko, A.R., Evans, A.J. and Raharjo, Y.C. 1985. Productivity of herded ducks in West Java.* Agric. Syst. *16: pp. 1–5)*

of rice bran or bananas and local protein sources such as fish, prawns and rats.

Conclusions

Fluctuating nutrient supplies are a problem in this system. Nomadism is a response to this constraint, but supplies of feeds other than fallow rice would increase egg output. Closer co-operation is also needed between duck and field owners to reduce the high death rate from insecticide poisoning.

Case study: The Office du Niger, Mali

The 'dead delta' of the Niger in central Mali is a fossil valley of the river, left dry when it changed its main course about 1000 BC. During the colonial period a dam was constructed at the confluence of the former and present channels to divert water into the old bed and the fossil valley was converted into an irrigation scheme. Small-scale farmers, known as *colons* or settlers (most of them forcibly transferred from their homes in Burkina Faso), were installed and set to growing cotton, in imitation of the Gezira scheme in the Sudan and to provide textile raw materials for metropolitan France. Following independence, the emphasis was put on food crop production and rice became the main crop.

The Office du Niger lies in the Sahel zone of Mali, with average annual rainfall of about 500 mm and temperatures of about 25 °C in the range 15–35 °C. Soils are alluvial clays with a poor drainage capacity and salinity is a major problem under irrigation. The scheme is organised in a series of villages with rainfed land surrounding it. Settlers, tenants of the Office in reality, cultivate rice under contract. Land holdings are constantly changing in area under a complicated system which takes account of family size; farm size, therefore, increases or decreases and there is no security of tenure. Farmers pay rent in the form of a percentage of the crop to the Office. Water and drainage changes are also levied on the crop. Although threshing would be more economical if done by the tenants it is done by the Office, which imposes a further levy. This is the only way that the Office can ensure that the crop will be delivered to it and not sold on the more lucrative open market.

Even though they are not natives of the area, most families have also set up dry-land farms on the periphery of the scheme where much of their labour is invested and where they grow crops, keep livestock and engage in the highly profitable trade in fuelwood for the nearby urban centre of Niono (Fig 4.3). The Office is effectively a monoculture of rice, but has hardly been touched by the 'green revolution', and only one crop of long-season varieties is grown per year. Land use efficiency is further reduced by uneven fields, silted irrigation canals and by the fact that tenants ensure that the drainage lines are higher than the

Fig 4.3   *Donkey cart loaded with fuel in the Niono area: central Mali*

surrounding land in order to obtain water for their private fields that lie outside the periphery of the scheme.

Most families own livestock. The principal species is cattle, owned by more than 90 per cent of households. Almost all families also own goats and more than half own sheep, although an inaccurate census by the Office claims that less than 20 per cent of families own one or both of these species. Donkeys are owned by about 60 per cent of families; all own domestic fowl; and many have Muscovy ducks and pigeons.

Individual holdings of cattle vary enormously from 1 head to 140 head although most holdings are small. The requirement for draught – and the availability of credit from the Office for the purchase of oxen – means that mature males dominate the structure of the herds and as many as 70 per cent of cattle are older draught oxen. Cattle gain weight very slowly due to poor nutrition and disease. Work oxen are not used for draught until they are 4–5 years old and then only for a limited number of seasons (Fig 4.4) partly because of chronic malnutrition leading to early senility and partly because credit is available to buy new animals.

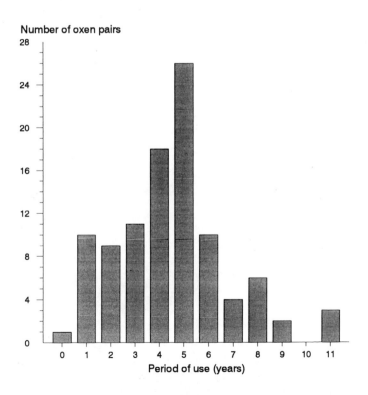

Fig 4.4 *Length of use of draught oxen in the Office du Niger, Mali*

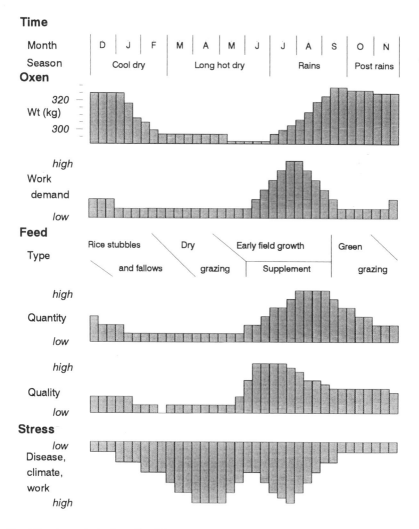

Fig 4.5 *An ecological profile of draught oxen in the Niono area, central Mali*

Goat flock sizes average about 9 head while sheep flocks are about 6 head. Both goats and sheep are kept mainly to provide meat, sheep especially being slaughtered at the main Islamic festivals. Goats are also milked to a limited extent. Flock structures are dominated by females (73 per cent) and young animals. Donkeys are used mainly for on- and off-farm transport and about 55 per cent of families own carts for this purpose: draught oxen are also used occasionally for transport, especially of crop residues. Fowl and ducks, as well as pigeons, are kept for meat rather than for eggs.

Livestock productivity could probably be improved. Work oxen are used for very few days in the year and are in their poorest condition when most labour is demanded of them (Fig 4.5). Cows produce 1 calf every 21 months and as many as 30 per cent of calves die before one year. Goats and sheep give birth about every 8 months, with litter sizes of 1.23 and 1.05, leading to annual reproductive rates of about 1.5 kids and 1.3 lambs. Male small ruminants are slaughtered for meat or sold at a young age but offtake is limited by the high preweaning mortality rates (30 per cent in goats and 25 per cent in sheep). Donkeys, in relation to the inputs provided and to their nutritional requirements, are the least understood but probably most economically productive animal species, with possible returns of 375 per cent/year for fuelwood transport and 600 per cent for those transporting building materials in urban centres. Livestock, exclusive of the value of draught power, contribute 15–20 per cent of total household revenue in this system.

Conclusions

There is considerable integration of crops and livestock.

- Cattle spend 43 per cent of total feeding time on crop residues, mainly rice, and other by-products are fed to them in their pens.
- Sheep and goats are confined and fed crop residues, or graze canal banks and regrowth or weeds in the fields.
- Poultry scavenge bran and broken rice grains and ducks feed on canal banks and on spilled grain in the fields.
- Donkeys are also fed crop residues and by-products.
- Cattle provide draught power and their feeding time on rice fields helps to maintain fertility since they deposit manure.

Small ruminants and poultry provide the protein supplement to the high-energy rice-based diet of their owners and, not being subject to levies by the Office, contribute to cash income when required. Cattle, and especially donkeys, transport the products of the fields and are also a source of cash in their off-farm transport activities.

Improvements in this system could be obtained by providing tenants with more secure land tenure. This would encourage them to invest in field and irrigation improvements, plant multi-purpose trees and integrate herbaceous legumes, in the long dead period induced by the single rice crop, to complement the low-quality straw. Credit in this system may possibly be counter-productive, allowing inefficient use of oxen.

5 Mixed smallholder farms in highland Africa

The system of mixed smallholder farms is typified in Africa by intensively cultivated areas at altitudes higher than 1500 m. Human population densities are usually also high. The main regions are in eastern Africa (Ethiopia, Kenya, part of Uganda and northern and southern Tanzania) and central Africa (Rwanda, Burundi, and Kivu and parts of Shaba Provinces in Zaire). Soils vary in origin but are mainly volcanic, with vertisols (black cracking clays) being common in Ethiopia and dark brown clay-loams in central Africa. Rainfall is generally bimodal, long and short rains and a long and short dry season, and annual rainfall generally exceeding 1000 mm, often by a large margin. Temperatures are moderated by the altitude, averaging about 22 °C all year round at 1500 m, and 15–18 °C at 2250 m, with occasional or frequent frosts at night at altitudes higher than 2500 m.

The main crops are annual subsistence ones, but cash crops are grown in some areas. Social factors affect the crops grown as much as, or more than, climate and soils. In Ethiopia teff (*Eragrostis abyssinica*) is used as the basis for *njera*, an unleavened bread that is the native food, but teff does not grow in all environments: wheat and barley are also grown, the last mainly for brewing of local beer: chick-peas, lentils, horsebeans (*Vicia faba*) and field peas, as well as very hot red peppers (used in the sauce that accompanies the *njera*) are also common crops. In central Africa bananas are the staple, coffee is widely grown by smallholders, and sweet potatoes, maize and haricot beans are also common.

The highlands are rarely considered to be important livestock areas, yet almost all families own ruminants and poultry. The large numbers of draught oxen, in conjunction with the intensive cropping, have led to severe land degradation in Ethiopia. Use of oxen is very inefficient in terms of hours worked and in power output but attempts to reduce pressure on feed resources by promoting the use of single ox ploughs (Fig 5.1) or the use of cows as work animals have been largely unsuccessful. Ethiopia has about 10 per cent of the world population of donkeys, most

Fig 5.1 *A single ox ploughing in Ethiopia*

of these being in the highlands, and large numbers of mules and horses. Sheep are very numerous and mainly used to provide meat at the major religious festivals of the Ethiopian Orthodox church in this ancient Christian country, although some wool is also taken from them. Goats are not common over most of the highlands but poultry are, as eggs are also eaten for religious reasons. In Kenya and in northern Tanzania small-scale dairying has been encouraged with use of crossbred and high grade cattle, mostly Ayrshire and Friesian. In central Africa cattle were important culturally in the past but the high human density (more than 600 people/km^2) has resulted in a great reduction in numbers. In the past there were taboos against eating mutton in some parts of Rwanda and Burundi, but these are fading and both goats and sheep are being encouraged by the political authorities and extension agents.

Animals are closely integrated in the whole system, particularly in Ethiopia where draught power is essential for cultivating the heavy soils. The lack of trees on the Ethiopian plateau unfortunately leads to the use, both at home and for sale, of animal manure as a fuel: as much as one third of cash income on some Ethiopian farms accrues from the sale of dung. As a result, there is a constant drain on the little remaining fertility of the already impoverished soils. More feed is available from crop residues and by-products than from natural grazing in Ethiopia, although neither of these sources is always fully or efficiently used for animal nutrition. In Ethiopia, animals are herded. In central Africa, cattle are herded but small ruminants are usually penned or attached individually to pickets on the farm or on roadside verges and are fed sweet potato vines and banana leaves among other farm products.

Case study: Rwanda, Burundi and Zaire

Almost all families own at least one species of ruminant and many own three. Individual holding sizes are very small, averaging less than 0.9 ha (of which 0.75 ha is cultivated to food crops) in most of the area although they are larger in the lower and drier areas. The number of animals owned is also small but varies to some extent, as does the mix of species, with altitude and rainfall (Table 5.1).

Table 5.1 Biophysical characteristics and livestock ownership patterns in highland central Africa

Region and Country	Altitude (m)	Rainfall (mm)	Temp. (°C)	Number of			
				Families	Cattle	Sheep	Goats
Bugorhe, Zaire	2000	1500	18	483	222	814	940
Giheta, Burundi	1700	1200	20	552	146	821	1232
Gashora, Rwanda	1300	1000	21	445	97	177	1682

Source: Bizimungu, A. 1986. *Productivité des petits ruminants en milieu rural. 1. Diagnostic de recensement-bétail dans trois régions différentes de la CEPGL.* Institut de Recherche Agronomique et Zootechnique: Gitega, Burundi

Bananas are by far the most important crop, cultivated by all families for home consumption and for sale. Bananas occupy about 40 per cent of the family farm, fruit yield about 9 t/year, and are grown mostly for beer (89.9 per cent), with cooking (8.1 per cent) and dessert (2.0 per cent) varieties being far less important. Haricot beans, cassava and sweet potatoes are almost always grown in association with bananas. The many minor crops include pigeon peas, maize, sorghum, various cucumbers and gourds, groundnuts, Irish potatoes and cocoyams or taro, and a great variety of green vegetables. The aim is to provide a constant supply of food throughout the year (Fig 5.2). A few trees (now mostly *Cupressus* and *Eucalyptus*) assure the supply of some fuel and coffee provides a cash income. Livestock are used for subsistence and to generate cash.

Cattle, once considered prestige animals, are now mainly kept for milk, male animals being sold for slaughter once they are well grown, usually at 3 or 4 years old. About 45 per cent of the small ruminant flock is under 15 months old and 27 per cent over three years: 82.0 per cent of the flock is female, 17.9 per cent males (almost all under 15 months of age) and 0.1 per cent older castrates.

Individual holdings of cattle are usually herded by day by a young family member and kept in a small enclosure close to the house at night. Small ruminants are permanently penned (27 per cent), attached

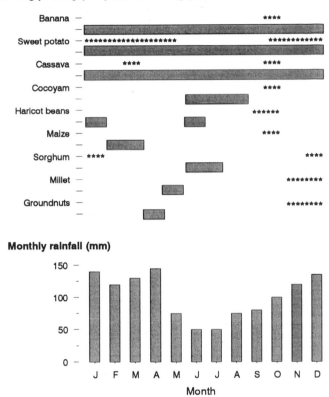

Sowing/planting (****) and harvesting (▨) activities

Banana	
Sweet potato	
Cassava	
Cocoyam	
Haricot beans	
Maize	
Sorghum	
Millet	
Groundnuts	

Monthly rainfall (mm)

150 —
100 —
50 —
0 —

J F M A M J J A S O N D

Month

Fig 5.2   *Rainfall and the agricultural calendar in highland central Africa*

Fig 5.3   *A goat attached to a picket in Rwanda*

individually (Fig 5.3) to pickets (58 per cent) or herded (15 per cent). About 84 per cent of goats and sheep are housed at night in the owner's residence, 9 per cent in a kitchen attached or close to the dwelling house and only 7 per cent in purpose-built enclosures.

Green fodder, supplementary to grazing, is provided by 49 per cent of owners, 33 per cent growing forage for this purpose with 16 per cent cutting natural grasses or weeds. Agricultural by-products are fed to animals by 72 per cent of owners. The type and amount of by-product varies seasonally, but 48 per cent of owners feed banana leaves (mostly in December to May in the short dry and rainy seasons), 25 per cent feed sweet potato vines and peelings (mostly in the long dry season of July to September), 7 per cent feed haricot beans and the remainder a variety of other products. Water for drinking is given to animals in pans or troughs by 44 per cent of owners, the remainder expecting their animals to use natural sources. Manure is carefully collected and spread directly on the arable land or composted with waste produce from the farm or house.

Conclusions

Constraints in this system are mainly related to pressure on land. Cultivation of steep slopes cleared of forest or woodland, without adequate anti-erosion measures, leads to rapid soil loss and associated effects. Lack of capital means that there is little in the way of farm infrastructure. Animal productivity in particular is well below optimum owing to poor extension services, inadequate veterinary support and a lack of market information. These problems are not insurmountable. If these services could be provided and coupled with the use of anti-erosion terraces for the growing of forage grasses and tree legumes such as *Leucaena leucocephala* to improve animal nutrition, then livestock output could be very considerably improved.

6 Mixed systems in the Latin American highlands

The mixed farm systems of Latin America systems have many features in common with similar systems in Africa. Human population density is high, pressure on land is intense and cultivation on steep slopes leads to severe degradation of resources. Holding sizes are small but not so fragmented as, for example, in the Kikuyu areas of Kenya.

Over such a large area, soils and rainfall vary tremendously. Soil type is not usually a major inhibitor of crop production and rainfall is normally in excess of 1000 mm/year and falls in a 6–8 month period, so a wide variety of crops can be grown. In some areas, none the less, night frosts occurring over several months may limit the range of crops that can be grown and prevent maximum use of the potential created by the high rainfall.

Most species of domestic livestock are found in the zone.

- Cattle provide milk, power and finally meat.
- Horses, mules and donkeys are used for draught and transport.
- Goats and, particularly, hair sheep are important in some areas.
- Pigs and poultry are used for food or to generate income.

Livestock may contribute up to 30 per cent of total income with cattle producing 60 per cent of the cash from all livestock. Animals are not only integrated with crops but amongst themselves, with pigs and poultry making use of whey from cheese manufacture.

In some areas farm labour is almost entirely provided by male members of the family, but in others both sexes contribute equally. In some specialised areas of the Latin American highlands, as in the Rio Negro area in Colombia, the use of labour on crops is so intensive that there is little available for animal care other than perhaps for a milk cow. Elsewhere there is generally good integration of agriculture and livestock.

Case study: The Central American highlands

Much of Central America consists of land over 1000 m in altitude with rainfall of 1000–2000 mm/year. The rain falls in an extended season from April to November. Precipitation and temperature are both favourable to the growing of a wide range of subsistence and cash crops. Soils do not limit agricultural operations, but steep slopes might.

Maize, a plant indigenous to this region, is the major crop on the generally small farms, which are usually less than 2 ha in size. Local varieties of maize are slow maturing, taking as much as nine months to ripen. The land is, therefore, intercropped with up to five other species, of which beans is the main one. Irish potatoes (which are also indigenous to the area), wheat and squash are also grown. Steep land is terraced to reduce erosion, and the resulting bunds provide livestock feed and material for compost, which is an important feature of the system.

The animal component of the complex usually includes one or a small number of cows, one or two pigs and, at higher altitudes, a small flock of sheep. Poultry are kept primarily for the production of eggs. Horses are a feature of this system with one horse to three farms on average. The staple foods are maize and beans, but livestock provide some products for consumption or for other forms of home use. Milk is drunk fresh or converted to cheese. Cattle born on the farm are kept to maturity at 5 years before being sold. Pigs are sold before they reach 12 months. The small amount of poor quality wool produced by the sheep is used to produce clothing and small handicraft items for sale.

There is a high degree of integration and interdependence among crops, animals and people. Animals are tethered during the growing season, when labour is devoted to crops, but are herded in the dry cold season. Dung is gathered and supplements crop waste in the compost pit. Crop residues and maize strippings provide animal feed in addition to grass from the bunded terraces. Feed resources away from the farm are limited because of population pressure which is also reducing wood for fuel. Equines are used to a limited extent to provide farm power but their main function is on- and off-farm transport.

Conclusions

There are many constraints in this system, including small farm size, population pressure, land tenure problems, distance from markets and poor transport infrastructure. Because of low incomes labour may have to be sold off the farm; on the other hand, landless people provide labour to farms in exchange for the right to cultivate a small plot.

7 Small farms in the lowland wetter tropics

The sub-humid and humid lowland tropics support high human population densities, are intensively cultivated with a variety of crops often producing more than one harvest per year, and can have high animal densities of various species. As in the irrigated systems, buffalo play a valuable role as do pigs and poultry.

The dominant crop or crops vary with the region. Upland, as well as paddy, rice is important everywhere, while maize and root crops such as yams, cocoyams, taro, cassava and sweet potatoes are more or less significant components of the cropping system according to the region. Fuel for cooking is a problem in some areas but not in others. Farms are characterised by a central homestead but their land may be either consolidated or fragmented. Farm infrastructure is often related to the degree of consolidation and includes terraces and bunds for water control and to a lesser extent for prevention of soil erosion.

Animals are well integrated with crops, but always pose a threat to them. Especially at the height of the growing season and approaching harvest, animals are subject to rigorous control, achieved through such methods as herding, tethering and fencing. Live fences of leguminous trees or shrubs like *Leucaena leucocephala* and *Gliricidia sepium* enhance soil fertility by nitrogen-fixation, provide mulch for crops, prevent animals from reaching crops (Fig 7.1) and produce a high-protein feed for livestock.

Conclusions

The advantages of these systems are the possibilities of multiple cropping, the feasibility of increasing high-value animal products and especially milk through closer integration of animals and crops and the development of co-operative grading and marketing of produce. Constraints include absence of credit, lack of animal health services, inefficient use of draught power and (with certain exceptions) poor marketing channels.

Fig 7.1 *A goat, fitted with a local collar, and a live* Leucaena *fence in Nigeria*

Case study: Small farm buffalo production in Sri Lanka

Sri Lanka is a tropical, mainly wet (minimum rainfall 1000 mm/year, maximum 4000 mm/year) country where 1.8 million smallholdings cover an area of 1.4 million ha. Average holding size is therefore about 0.78 ha but there are also additional areas used communally to graze livestock and for other purposes including gathering fuel. Many people do not own any land but have access to unfarmed areas for grazing and for wild products. Many others cultivate rice on state-owned land. In the rural areas 80–95 per cent of the population are under 45 years old but 25 per cent are illiterate. Upland rice is a major smallholder crop of which some is sold and the remainder used for home consumption, to repay loans, and given to landlords in lieu of rent. Subsidiary annual food crops include cowpea, green gram and groundnut and the homesteads are planted with coconut, jackfruit, mango, banana and citrus. In contrast to many tropical areas, a majority of farmers use chemical fertilisers to increase rice yields.

The main livestock species are buffalo, cattle (75 per cent of families owning buffalo also keep cattle) and poultry, with goats being a very minor component (4 per cent of farmers). Cattle are kept in small numbers to produce milk, with a single lactation providing a yield of 1500–2500 kg. Poultry are also few and provide each family with 350–500 eggs/year. Buffalo herd sizes vary with agro-ecological zone, from 5.5 ± 6.3 head in the wet middle altitudes to 22.7 ± 36.1 in the low areas. The large standard deviation indicates the great variation in individual herd sizes.

Buffalo are kept solely for draught purposes by 64 per cent of owners, for draught and milk by 35 per cent, and for milk and other purposes (puddling clay for bricks, expressing oil from coconuts and as power

Table 7.1 Population structure (per cent) of buffalo herds in the humid tropics in Sri Lanka

Age or class	Male	Sex	Female
		Male		**Female**
< 1 year		17.1	
1–2 years		13.0	
Heifers > 2 years	–		9.1
Mature cows	–		32.8
Mature males	13.1		–
Mature castrates	14.9		–
All animals	44.2		55.8

Source: data from Perera, B.M.A.O. and Silva, L.N.A. 1986. Small farm buffalo production in Sri Lanka. In: Chantalakhana, C. (ed), *Proceedings of the buffalo seminar, April 29–May 2, 1985*. International Buffalo Center: Bangkok, Thailand: pp. 59–75

sources on wells) by a small minority. Buffalo are kept primarily for home use with only 12.3 per cent of farmers regularly using them to obtain cash income. The predominance of draught use affects herd structure, there being 4 males for every 5 females in the herd (Table 7.1). Buffalo cows are milked for only 2–3 months in most cases. Age at first calving is 45.7 months and the annual calving rate is 61.4 per cent, giving a calving interval of 18.9 months and a total of 6–9 calves in a life of 20.5 years. There is a marked peak in calving in January, with 60 per cent of all births taking place in December to February. Management practices affect reproductive performance, this being better than the average in herds where only partial suckling is allowed, which are milked, and which are not used for work. Annual mortality rates are 25 per cent to 1 year, 21 per cent in the age group 1–2 years and 8 per cent in older animals. Internal parasites and haemorrhagic septicaemia are major health problems.

Feeding management consists mainly of free-range grazing, with 71 per cent of farmers using this system either alone or in combination with tethering. Tethering only is practised by 29 per cent of farmers. In addition 12 per cent of farmers cut and carry grass for their animals, 15 per cent feed rice straw in the wet season and 31 per cent do so in the dry season. Buffalo are first used for work at 3 years, when some males are also castrated, and have a working life of 18 years. The working day is 6–8 hours ploughing or puddling land for 30–60 days/year, and 83 per cent of farmers use both sexes of buffalo for this work. Ploughing occupies buffalo 11.6 days/ha, puddling 32.6 days and levelling 6.7 days.

44

Threshing by trampling occupies buffaloes 8–11 hours/day for 12–46 days and requires 21.7 buffalo days/ha. Animals also wallow about 2 hours/day.

Conclusions

There is very close integration between animals and crops in this system, particularly in the use of buffalo to provide power and manure and the crop residues or by-products provided to the buffalo. The major constraint identified is the expansion of irrigated rice cultivation and the creation of settlement schemes, both of which are reducing the fallow and semi-jungle areas which have in the past provided a large proportion of buffalo feed. The low reproductive rate and the high mortality of buffalo are other constraints. The technical solutions to these problems are known but multi-disciplinary studies are required to identify the reasons for them not being successfully applied. Some possible reasons are expense, too heavy demands on labour and social inhibitions.

Case study: Trypanotolerant livestock in The Gambia

Tsetse flies infest approximately 10 million km^2 or about 40 per cent of Africa. The *Glossina* species of fly are the vectors of trypanosomiasis, which hinders agricultural development and causes poor weight gains, stunted growth, lowered milk production and reproductive disorders in livestock. Trypanosomiasis affects 39 African countries to varying degrees. Besides losses of meat and milk, trypanosomiasis limits land utilisation in infested areas and may lead to overgrazing in non-infested areas. Africa's tsetse-infested savannas are the region's only remaining land source with good physical and biological potential, representing much of the best watered and most fertile land on the continent.

The Gambia has the second highest cattle density in Africa and by far the highest in West Africa. Numbers of sheep and goats are estimated at 120 841 and 179 653. The vast majority of cattle are of the trypanotolerant N'Dama breed which, together with other trypanotolerant breeds of *Bos taurus* cattle, is also prevalent throughout much of the tsetse-infested areas of humid and sub-humid West Africa. Sheep are mainly of the small-framed Djallonké type and goats are of the West African Dwarf type: both of these groups are trypanotolerant to a greater or lesser degree. Two tsetse species, *Glossina palpalis* and *G. morsitans*, occur in The Gambia, both of which are near the northern limit of their distribution. Nowhere in The Gambia is more than 20 km from a tsetse area and all livestock are exposed to challenge.

Cultivated and fallow areas increased from 17.6 per cent to 47.4 per cent during 1946–1981/1983, representing a major decline in the area of wet season grazing available to livestock. At the same time, however, the amount of crop residues available to livestock increased. In 1991 these were estimated at 130 000 t of groundnut haulm, 66 000 t of millet plus sorghum stover, 19 000 t of maize stover and 13 000 t of rice straw.

Bush forage represents 80 per cent of dry-season fodder for livestock, but this can be depleted by uncontrolled bush fires. The remaining 20 per cent comprises various crop residues. Upland cereal stovers and rice stubble are grazed after the harvest early in the dry season. Cereal residues are not stored but 70 per cent of households dry and store groundnut hay, which is fed to selected groups of livestock throughout the dry season. Residues from village processing, such as sesame cake, and cereal brans are potentially valuable livestock feeds. Improved nutrition is of major importance as it contributes to the ability to resist disease, including trypanosomiasis.

About one third of households own cattle, the mean number per owner being usually over 10. Most of the cattle belong to a few 'wealthy' people. Widespread ownership of draught animals emphasises their importance for tillage. Ownership of small ruminants by a majority of households underlines their often underestimated role in the rural economy. Participation by women in sheep and goat ownership is 37 per cent and 51 per cent. Average flock sizes in four localities in 1986 were 5.2 for sheep only, 6.5 for goats only and 16.8 for a mixture of sheep and goats.

The main cash income for most households is from crop sales. While income from livestock appears to be relatively small, animals, nevertheless, make a major contribution to the rural economy. The major reasons for owning small ruminants are for use in religious ceremonies and as a repository of wealth. Sheep and goats are readily exchangeable for cash or cattle. Most farmers, however, only dispose of animals when they are really in need of money. Infertile and old females and male lambs and kids are the first to be sold or slaughtered. The best male sheep are, however, the main category traded. They are slaughtered for the major Islamic festival of *Id-el-Kabir*, celebrated by 90 per cent of The Gambian people.

Utilisation of livestock products is surprisingly low. The consumption of beef has been estimated at 4.2–5.3 kg/person/year. Per capita milk availability varies from 21 cm^3 to 295 cm^3 daily. Fish, meat and dairy products contribute little to the total energy intake of either urban or rural communities (Table 7.2). Consumption of animal products is largely governed by market prices. A critical factor in depressing the demand for meat is its relatively high cost which, in May/June 1991, was ten times that of a local sea fish.

Grazing intensity is uneven, being most severe around the villages

Table 7.2 Energy intake per person and expenditure on various goods in The Gambia

Energy source	Type of household			
	Urban		Rural	
	kJ	% expenditure	kJ	% expenditure
Meat	129	6.1	138	6.4
Dairy products	310	6.5	247	5.5
Fish	736	9.8	603	10.4
Other	10 447	77.6	9 552	77.7
Total intake	11 622		10 540	

where animals are tethered and/or watered. There are striking changes in dietary intake and stocking densities because of seasonal migrations to and from riverine flood plains where there are very high tsetse fly densities. Grazed areas and daily grazing ambits are maximal during the late dry season (April–June) when bush forage is poor. During the rains, areas and distances are smaller. During the early dry season, much time is spent grazing crop residues close to the villages. Feed intake of cattle (Fig 7.2) reflects clear seasonal changes.

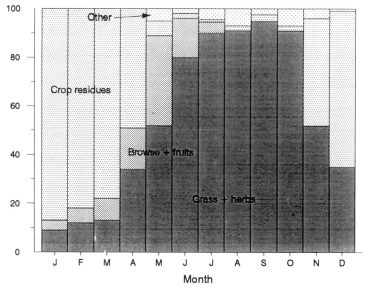

Fig 7.2 *Seasonal intake of various diet components by cattle in The Gambia*

Where farmers own both sheep and goats, they are usually kept together in the compound in small huts made of earth bricks or split rhun palm (*Borassus aethiopicum*), roofed with palm leaves. During the non-cropping season, small ruminants leave the hut as early as 06.00 hours to graze on communal pastures 1–2 km away from the compound and return at midday and at dusk. Feed supplements, such as groundnut hay and millet and sorghum brans, are usually given to fattening male sheep only before major religious festivals. During the cropping season, sheep and goats usually remain confined inside the compound for most of the day and are only grazed nearby, while tethered, for a few hours daily. Alternatively, a contract herdsman or group of young boys supervise large flocks (100 animals) in uncultivated areas during the afternoon. The animals are kept hungry in the morning so that they remain more manageable and are less apt to wander during the afternoon grazing.

The prevalence of trypanosomiasis (per cent animals infected) varies from area to area but is generally highest after the rains. Differences are explained by local challenge levels, seasonal changes in cattle density and the contact rate between cattle and tsetse flies. Tick burdens on cattle are generally low.

Unrestricted breeding allows cattle to calve throughout the year but 80 per cent of calves are born in July to December. This seasonality is related to the availability of feed from September onwards, towards the end of the previous year's rainy season. Calving intervals average about 21 months with a lactation length of 14 months. Cattle productivity indexes, based on weight gain, milk production and young and adult mortality, are equivalent to about 75 kg of weaned calf/cow/year.

Lambing and kidding in sheep and goats take place throughout the year with a peak in December for both species. Most conceptions thus occur in the early wet season, which is marked by a rapid increase in feed availability. Average litter sizes are 1.15 for sheep and 1.30 for goats. With a parturition interval of 11.1 months for sheep and a lamb live weight of 11.5 kg at 3–4 months, the total weight of weaned lamb (3–4 months old) is about 12.4 kg/ewe/year . Goats produce about 11.0 kg of weaned kid/doe/year.

Conclusions

The major constraints in this system are the presence of trypanosomiasis, the high stocking rates (although this is rarely a problem in other parts of the tsetse-infested zone) and the seasonal nature of the feed supply. Poor prices for livestock and their products are another constraint, except when rams are sold for the major Islamic feasts. Local livestock are, however, relatively well adapted to the environment and would probably outperform other types of stock under similar levels of management. They are already well integrated into the overall agricultural system via draught power and the use of crop residues. The trypanotolerance trait is important in maintaining the overall sustainability of the system as it reduces the need for tsetse fly control and the use of trypanocides. Trypanotolerance is thus an environmentally friendly as well as an important economic trait as it reduces chemical pollution and avoids the build-up of resistance in trypanosomes. Livestock production would be enhanced by the provision of better protection from cheap and subsidised foreign competition and the delivery of better livestock extension advice.

8 Tree crop systems

Systems which integrate tree crops with livestock are known as sylvo-pastoral, while those including annual or perennial ground crops as well are termed agro-sylvo-pastoral. Different kinds of system with a sylvicultural component can be identified (Fig 8.1), including those in which natural forests or woodlands are a major source of feed, and those in which feed is from tree forages planted specifically or mainly for this purpose. Both these types of system have been mentioned in previous chapters, this chapter will concentrate on systems which include major plantation tree crops.

The major plantation crops occupy land for as long as 50 years and there are invariably periods at which they are unproductive or not fully productive. Advantages to the crop of closer integration with livestock would appear to be increased soil fertility through return of dung and urine; control of weeds and reduced use of chemical herbicides and labour; and, ultimately, higher total yields of crop (not least because of greater recovery rates of, for example, coconut where 90 per cent of fallen nuts can be gathered in systems where livestock are available for transport, as against 75 per cent in systems without livestock). Advantages to the animal are a greater total availability of feed and a more gentle climate under shade, which may allow greater levels of production from existing genotypes or even the introduction of higher performing genotypes. There may also be shared advantages, especially if leguminous forages are grown in the plantation, and the combined product output from trees and animals may be greater.

Plantation crops cover large areas of land not always suitable for short-term arable cropping. They include coconut, oil palm, rubber, cocoa, sago and tropical fruits in the humid zones and dates under irrigation in the drier zones. Coconut is grown on more than 7 million ha, mostly in Asia, and rubber is also important there. Oil palms are found throughout much of the wet tropics including West Africa, where there are also large areas of cocoa and coconut (Fig 8.2). By-products from plantation crops have long been used as livestock feed, often in countries far away from the source because processing has been concentrated in the major

(a) Shea butter nut (*Butyrospermum paradoxum*) and Locust bean (*Parkia biglobosa*) grown for fodder and as a cash crop in sub-humid Mali.

(b) *Pinus pinnata* grown as an anti-erosion crop and for fuel in highland Burundi.

Fig 8.1   *Tree crops*

Fig 8.2   *Coconut/cattle system in coastal Benin in West Africa*

industrialised countries. Many by-products are now being used locally and there are attempts to use new and unconventional ones. Some of these have poor nutritional value (Table 8.1) unless they are specially treated, but modern technology such as treatment with ammonia compounds or the use of radiation can improve feed values.

Not all forage crops are equally suitable companions for each plantation crop, since plantation crops vary in height and shade and also because of nitrogen requirements. Under coconut palms grazed by cattle in Asia and Oceania an induced ground cover of *Paspalum* grass and *Desmodium* and *Indigofera* legumes can develop, although this may become dominated by the unproductive *Mimosa pudica* or *M. invisa.* Planted grasses of the genera *Brachiaria* and *Digitaria* and *Panicum maximum* do well in this environment, while *Centrosema pubescens* may also be a useful legume. Under oil palm, legumes including *C.pubescens*, *Calopogonium mucunoides* and *Stylosanthes* spp. do better than grasses, but productivity is much reduced at about eight years as the palm canopy becomes complete. Similar problems of canopy closure are encountered in rubber, where a semi-natural poorly productive ground cover of lalang (*Imperata cylindrica*), Siam weed (*Eupatorium odoratum*) and *Mimosa pudica* develops.

Table 8.1 Proximate composition and nutritional values of some tree plantation crops and other agro-industrial by-products

By-product	Dry matter (%)	Composition (% of dry matter)					TDN (% DM)	Metabolizable energy (MJ/kg)
		Protein	Fat	Fibre	NDF	ADF		
Coconut cake	90.8	18.0	10.2	13.2	–	20.0	77	11.5
Palm kernel cake (solvent)	91.0	17.6	0.9	15.6	70.5	40.0	70	10.0
Palm kernel cake (expeller)	81.1	15.0	10.6	16.8	69.7	39.6	71	10.0
Palm oil mill effluent	93.3	10.6	13.0	17.9	–	–	68	9.8
Palm press fibre	72.6	7.9	9.4	40.7	75.4	52.8	48	7.3
Mango leaves	45.2	9.3	4.6	24.1	39.2	34.0	–	–
Shaora (*Streblus asper*) leaves	34.6	17.7	2.9	16.3	37.4	30.9	–	–
Sago refuse	27.0	1.5	2.0	10.0	–	14.5	–	11.5
Cocoa pod husk	89.5	6.8	1.2	29.1	–	42.0	44	8.5
Cocoa shell[1]	90.7	21.2	2.5	12.8	–	–	–	17.8
Pineapple waste	12.0	6.5	1.2	18.0	–	37.0	64	10.1
Sisal pulp	–	5.3	3.1	29.0	–	–	55	–
Sisal bagasse	–	5.3	3.7	28.0	–	–	55	–
Kapok seed meal (expeller)	90.0	31.0	8.0	30.0	–	–	–	–
Kapok oil cake	95.4	32.8	7.0	22.3	–	–	–	–
Rice bran	91.0	13.5	12.2	13.0	30.0	18.0	76	11.5
Wheat bran	89.0	14.8	4.0	10.0	41.8	12.5	62	11.2
Poultry manure	36.0	28.0	4.0	21.0	–	16.0	52	7.9

Note:
1 Net energy value in last column
2 NDF = neutral-detergent fibre; ADF = acid-detergent fibre; TDN = total digestible nutrients; DM = dry matter

Source: Jalaludin, S. 1989. Ruminant feeding systems in Southeast Asia. In: *Feeding strategies for improving productivity of ruminant livestock in Developing Countries (Panel Proceedings Series STI/PUB/823)*. International Atomic Energy Agency: Vienna, Austria: pp. 31–50 [with some additional data]

Conclusions

A major problem in all plantation systems is the availability of forage which fluctuates greatly through the life cycle of the trees. In the first 3–5 years it may not be possible to graze livestock in the plantation because of potential damage to the main crop. From the eighth year the closure of the canopy again reduces productivity. In spite of these difficulties the potential for much greater integration of trees with livestock is excellent. Tree planting cycles can be geared to feed production, and planting geometry can be modified to help obtain higher forage yields. However, the returns from animal production need to be sufficient to offset any possible reduction in yield from the plantation.

Case study: Draught buffalo in Malaysian oil palm plantations

The oil palm industry is extremely labour intensive but presumably profitable, as the area under this crop in the Malaysian Federation expanded from 755 525 ha in 1978 to 1 369 269 ha in 1988. The increase in area led to a labour shortage for the heavy and tedious jobs of cutting and particularly of carrying the fruit bunches to specified roadside locations. The fruit has traditionally been carried to the roadside, two bunches at a time, on a shoulder yoke. In order to overcome the shortage of labour different owners have tried mini-tractors, bicycles, wheelbarrows and buffalo carts. Young buffalo approaching 2 years and weighing about 200 kg, as well as carts, have been provided to labourers who repay the purchase price from their wages over a period of time. The labourer is also responsible for training, feeding and care of his animal. The use of carts is much more efficient than other methods of transport. The carts carry about 500 kg of fruit at each trip and about five loads a day cover the labourer's allotted task. Buffalo graze in the plantation while cutting is going on and between loads but also in the afternoons as the use of carts reduces the time taken to complete the task.

Buffalo clearly find adequate feed from grazing alone as growth rates of young animals are comparable to animals of similar weight and age on research stations. Supplementary feeding with cut grass or a commercial concentrate does not lead to better daily gains. Metabolisable energy intake by working buffalo (Table 8.2) is about 1.7 times that required for maintenance alone in lighter animals and almost 1.5 times the maintenance requirement in animals near mature weight.

Conclusions

Integration of buffalo in this system has resulted in an increase in the market value of the oil palm, an increase in labour productivity of 31 per

Table 8.2 Weight, dry matter intake and metabolisable energy intake, utilisation and balance by buffalo on oil palm estates in Malaysia

Buffalo age group	Live weight (kg)	Dry matter intake (kg)	Metabolisable energy (KJ/kg$^{0.75}$)				
				Utilisation			
			Intake	Maintenance	Draught	Walking	Balance
Growing	305	8.52	958.8	554.0	41.9	17.4	345.5
Near mature	435	9.36	807.0	554.0	45.7	18.5	188.8
Overall	348	8.94	882.9	554.0	43.8	18.0	267.2

Source: Liang, J.B., Nasir, A.M., Ismail, A. and Abdullah, R.S. 1989. Management of draught animals in Malaysian oil palm estates. In: Hoffmann, D., Nari, J. and Petheram, R.J. (eds), *Draught animals in rural development.* Australian Centre for International Agricultural Research: Canberra, Australia: pp. 242–245

cent coupled with a reduction in labour requirement of 23 per cent, and significantly reduced costs for weeding. Total estate productivity would undoubtedly be further increased if buffalo were bred on the farm and if females were used to produce milk as well as providing transport.

Case study: Beef under coconut palm in the Solomon Islands

Cattle introduced into commercial copra plantations in the South Pacific have multiple advantages. They reduce weeding costs, increase copra production (mainly through greater recovery rates) and provide additional income from the sale of beef. Problems encountered relate to adjusting the animal stocking rate to the required amount, and to availability of ground vegetation, which in turn is governed by soil fertility, the amount of shade produced by tree density and age, topography, rainfall and season. Overstocking can lead to compacted soils and damage to trees and pasture, while understocking results in inadequate control of undergrowth, leading to a lower percentage of nut recovery and suppressed palm growth.

Over the years it has been shown that cattle at 1.0–1.5 livestock equivalents per hectare increase nut pick-up from 75 per cent to 90 per cent and lead to total labour requirements that are 50 per cent less than when there are no cattle. At the same time, copra yields increase by as much as 30 per cent and total profitability by up to 200 per cent.

9 Agro-pastoral systems in the semi-arid tropics

The semi-arid tropics are found principally in two belts, one north and one south of the equator. Semi-arid areas are located mainly on the major land masses (in Africa, western Asia, Indian, central and South America, northern Australia) but some oceanic islands (generally small, but Madagascar is a notable exception) also have semi-arid climates. A semi-arid climate may be defined in several ways. Annual rainfall of 250 mm to as much as 1000 mm is one definition; a growing period of 75 or 90 days to 150 or 180 days is another. All semi-arid climates are characterised by markedly seasonal conditions, with a single short rainy season (although parts of East Africa have bimodal rainfall) of 3 to 5 months and a long dry season, part of which is very hot.

In the semi-arid tropics livestock are an important component of farming systems. An agro-pastoral system can be defined as one in which between 10 per cent and 50 per cent of total household revenue (the value of home consumption plus income) derives from livestock or livestock products. Sales of animals, meat, milk, fibres, skins and any cash earned (for example, by livestock transport operations) are included in the contribution of livestock revenue.

The harsh conditions in this agro-ecological zone require that crops, as well as animals, be hardy and adaptable. The major cereal crops are 'millets' (including *Pennisetum* and *Digitaria*) and sorghums. The collection of seeds from wild grasses, such as *Cenchrus* and non-cultivated species of *Digitaria,* is a common strategy used to supplement grain production, particularly in dry years and in longer droughts. Food legumes such as cowpea, and groundnut in the better areas, are grown, as are a variety of condiments (peppers and spices) and vegetables (okra, egg plant and tomato), the last particularly close to the village or home compound, where some water may be used and where manure from animals' night accommodation can be applied.

The range of animals kept in semi-arid agro-pastoral systems is perhaps wider than in any other climatic zone or farming system. In South

America species include llama, alpaca, cattle, sheep, goats, pigs, equines and poultry. In Africa the South American Camelidae are replaced by the one-humped or Arabian camel and there are very few pigs, mainly because of the Islamic prohibition on the eating of their flesh. Dogs are kept for meat by some animistic tribes in parts of West Africa. In India buffalo can be added to the list, and the yak in Nepal. Fish are allowed to multiply in many river and floodplain areas but may also be farmed to some extent by the use of trenches, ponds or permanent netting or other types of enclosures. Honey from wild bees is also important in some areas; again, the bees may be farmed using hives.

Animals and crops are often well integrated in this system. Cattle, Camelidae (Fig 9.1), Equidae and buffalo are all used for draught power and are usually important suppliers of milk. Goats and sheep produce mainly meat, but their milk and fibres often contribute considerably to household subsistence and to cash income. Manure from every species is used to restore fertility to cropped land. Hides and skins are used for tents and as containers (Fig 9.2). Crop residues and by-products are major sources of feed for animals.

Fig 9.1 *Camels ploughing river terraces under* Acacia albida *trees at Zalingei in the Jebel Mara district, Sudan*

57

Fig 9.2 *Donkeys with goat skins slung under their bellies as water containers in north Maradi, Niger*

Case study: The Baqqara transhumant system in western Sudan

The Baqqara (from the Arabic *baqqar* for cattle) are a group comprising some 15 tribes occupying much of central-west Sudan between 10 °N and 14 °N latitude. The climate is semi-arid to arid with rainfall of 300–600 mm/year, decreasing from south to north. The wet season is very short and much of the rain falls in concentrated heavy storms, often leading to high losses caused by run-off. Dry-season temperatures exceed 40 °C and these, coupled with increasing humidity as the rains approach, create very stressful conditions for both people and animals.

Four major land units can be distinguished, each having its major soil type and associated vegetation patterns.

- The Basement Complex – thin eroded soils with little water-holding capacity. Here ground cover is sparse, consisting mainly of annual grasses and thorny acacias, particularly *Acacia nubica* and *A. mellifera*, while the baobab or *tebeldi* (*Adansonia digitata*) is the dominant upper storey tree.
- *Nagaa* – an area of non-cracking clays which are waterlogged during the rains and very hard and dry in the long dry season. *Acacia seyal* is a major thorny shrub on this soil type, often in association with *Balanites aegyptiaca.*
- *Qoz* – an area of formerly mobile sand dunes now fixed by growth of large trees. Most of the woody species on all three land units are valuable browse plants and provide much of the livestock feed in the dry season, when the annual grasses have dried off and been eaten or blown away.

- *Bahr* (Arabic for sea) or *wadi* – characterised by higher productivity due to the presence of seasonal water courses which ensure a perennial or almost perennial supply of sub-surface water at shallow depth in the alluvial soils. This allows the growth of crops, grasses and trees over extended periods: *Acacia albida* is a major multi-purpose tree in this unit.

The major crop is bulrush millet (*Pennisetum typhoides*) of which several local short- and long-season cultivars are grown. In normal years average yields of millet are about 800 kg/ha, but crop failures are frequent, apparently more so in the last two decades. Sorghum (*Sorghum bicolor*) is an important crop in the *bahr* (*wadi*) units and as a post-rains crop on the *nagaa*: yields of 2000 kg/ha are not unusual but the area grown is small compared with millet. Groundnuts are grown on relatively large areas on most land units. Several vegetables and condiments are planted on suitable soils, particularly where micro-irrigation is possible.

As the ethnic group name Baqqara suggests, cattle are the principal animal species. Herd sizes per herding unit average 106 head and about 80 per cent of herds have 50–150 cattle. Females represent 69 per cent of total numbers and cows of breeding age make up 43 per cent of the herd. Cattle produce less meat than the other ruminants and camels (Table 9.1), but herds which migrate regularly are about 50 per cent

Table 9.1 Livestock production parameters for five domestic species in the Baqqara system, Sudan

Parameter	Species				
	Cattle	**Goat**	**Sheep**	**Camel**	**Donkey**
Herd structure					
Males, total (%)	31.2	23.6	22.2	50.0	51.4
breeding (%)	4.2	5.2	8.4	?	37.0
Females, total (%)	68.8	76.4	77.8	50.0	48.6
breeding (%)	42.8	49.8	57.0	30.0	31.8
Vital statistics					
Birth rate (young/female/year)	0.49	2.08	1.45	0.70	0.65
Death rate (%/year)	19	19	23	15	?
Offtake (sales + consumption, %/year)	16	28	26	15	n.a.
Breeding female weight (kg)	300	30	40	414	120
Productivity					
Dressing percentage	45	49	41	49	n.a.
Index (g meat/female/year)	44	374	253	67	n.a.

Sources: Wilson, R.T., Bailey, L., Hales, J., Moles, D. and Watkins, A.E. 1980. The cultivation-cattle complex in Western Darfur. *Agric. Syst.* 5: pp. 119–135; and Wilson, R.T. and Clarke, S.E. 1975. Studies on the livestock of Southern Darfur, Sudan. I. The ecology and livestock resources of the area. *Trop. Anim. Hlth. Prod.* 7: pp. 165–187

more productive than sedentary ones. Cattle are kept principally for milk which is drunk fresh, in tea, and converted into butter. Entire bulls and castrates are also used as pack animals.

Sheep and goats are of similar importance. Sheep flocks average about 43 head and goat flocks are probably about the same, although the latter are often owned by several people, including women and children, and absolute ownership is difficult to establish. Females account for more than three animals out of four in both species. The Sudan Desert sheep are large animals and are kept primarily for home slaughter at Islamic festivals or for offering hospitality to guests. The Sudan Desert goat is also a large animal, highly prolific and a good milk producer. Young males are slaughtered early and eaten mainly by the household.

Equines are common in this system, horses being used solely for riding, donkeys as riding and pack animals and occasionally to draw water carts. Some Baqqara own a camel for transport purposes. Almost all families keep domestic fowl, even those which migrate long distances regularly. Averaging 40 g each about 50 eggs/hen/year are produced, but the death rate, especially from Newcastle Disease in the winter, is appallingly high. Pigeons, which are of general importance to most Muslims as food, are kept by almost all sedentary families and in the base villages of the migratory sections of the population.

Livestock, people, cropped areas and natural bush are closely integrated and interdependent in the Baqqara system. Aerial surveys have shown that the distribution of livestock is positively correlated with cultivated areas in the dry season, indicating that crop residues are an important feed source at this time. Conversely, there is a negative correlation between stock and crops in the rains as animals migrate away from the cultivated areas. The only exception is goats, which stay close to the women and children, who remain in the villages. In the mid-1970s the field layer was estimated to provide some 75 per cent, crop residues 14 per cent and browse 11 per cent of the 2.5 t of energy available per livestock unit per year. The contributions of the three sources were 56 per cent, 9 per cent and 35 per cent of the 160 kg of total protein available. Livestock return manure to the crop sub-sector and provide transport from field to homestead and from there to market. In addition, donkeys and oxen are indispensable for transport on the frequent long- and short-distance moves of the camping unit (Fig 9.3).

Conclusions

Various problems have arisen in recent decades. Mass vaccination campaigns against rinderpest, contagious bovine pleuro-pneumonia and other diseases have been relatively successful and allowed an increase in the number of stock to well above the carrying capacity of the feed

Fig 9.3 *Ox used as riding and pack animal in the Baqqara system in Darfur, Sudan*

resources. Political demands by the Baqqara for new areas to be made available for dry-season grazing through the sinking of deep bores have laid waste vast areas of rangeland. Drought and famine in northern Darfur and civil unrest in Darfur and Chad to the west have led to enormous influxes of refugees, all of whom have occupied and cultivated land unsuitable for such use, while their livestock have imposed intolerable pressure on an already fragile resource base. This disastrous sequence of events is now a well documented and world renowned catastrophe from which the area may never recover.

Case study: Mixed cropping in India

In the semi-arid area of Gujarat State, small farms are highly fragmented and there is little incentive for owners to invest in improved animal production. Herding is rarely done and animals rove at will, especially during the dry season. Because of fragmentation, labour requirements for collecting and feeding crop residues are high. Many animal owners have no land but make up to 90 per cent of their income by using their animals to transport other people's produce.

Arable areas comprise mixed plantings or intercropping for subsistence and some monoculture of cash crops. Food crops, however, predominate and these are grown with few capital or other inputs. Crops are usually planted after the monsoon, especially on heavy cracking clays, which are fallowed during the rains. Increasing population pressure has led to increased areas of crops, reducing the fallow phase and limiting the

61

amount of wood available for fuel and building. Most cattle and buffalo manure is therefore converted to fuel for home use or for sale. Sales of this commodity can account for 60 per cent of cash income. Animal dung is also used for building.

This system is unusual in that cattle are preferred for draught and buffalo for milk. The better off farmers own a pair of bullocks. The two to four each of goats, sheep and poultry per household are managed by women. All these animals and their products are sold to generate cash. Animal feed is almost entirely crop residues, by-products such as bran from home processing of grain, and field weeds, with some roadside grazing. The long, hot dry season before the monsoon is a time of feed and water shortage and heavy weight losses occur, rendering animals unfit for ploughing when they are most needed.

Conclusions

Much of the high but erratic seasonal rainfall is lost through run-off. It appears that traditional water management practices are conducive to soil erosion and the cultivation implements used are inefficient in their use of power. Improved water management and better implements, especially for minimum tillage, would improve both crop and animal performance.

Case study: The sertao of Ceara State, north-east Brazil

North-east Brazil comprises 20 per cent of the country's land area and has 18 per cent of its cattle, 92 per cent of its goats, 34 per cent of its sheep, 23 per cent of its pigs and 67 per cent of its donkeys and mules. The *sertao* is the region's hottest area, with a dense cover of shrubs, and shallow stony soils. It has complex climatic, vegetational and soil inter-relationships. Altitude varies from 100 m to 300 m. Annual rainfall is in the band 450–850 mm, falling mostly (93 per cent) in a 5 month period in January–June. The climate is thus of the classic semi-arid monomodal tropical type. The area is subject to recurrent short- and long-term droughts, one of which occurred in 1980–1983. Farm size is very variable (18–450 ha) but considerably larger than most farms in Africa and Asia.

Farmers use a traditional soil classification, based on features which determine suitability for crop production. Preferred soils are alluvial deposits (*coroas* or *baixios* in local terminology) with the sandy types (*ariscado*) preferred over clayey ones (*liguento, massape*) because of freer drainage and ease of cultivation. Red clays (*barro vermelho*) are less favoured as they are relatively sticky and are found on rolling terrain. The seasonally waterlogged *tabuleiro* and the dark cracking *massape* soils provide good grazing. Here soil/water relationships hinder the growth of woody plants but produce a good herbaceous layer.

Vegetation types are known collectively as *caatinga*. Most woody species are deciduous and their fallen leaves are an important component of livestock feed in the long dry season. The four principal sub-types within the main one are arboreal, shrubby, open woodland and palm. Arboreal *caatinga* has been relatively little disturbed and comprises species of *Piptadenia*, *Tabebuia*, *Caesalpinia* and *Schinus*. Shrubby *caatinga* has either been disturbed by slash-and-burn agriculture or is on poor quality sites and has a dense, 3–6 m high, woody layer of *Combretum*, *Mimosa* and *Jatropha* spp. with *Croton hermiargyeus* being a major invader on account of its ability to spread rapidly in poor soils. Open woodland is found on poorly drained sites and has species similar to the shrubby type as well as species of *Cnidoscolus* and *Pilocereus* on drier sites. Palm stands occur on soils subject to periodic flooding, the palm itself being *Copernicia cerifera*, which also produces the multi-purpose carnauba wax.

Successful farming in this area depends on an ability to shift resources from crops to livestock and vice versa in response to fluctuating conditions. As many as 20 different crop combinations have been identified. The main food crops are maize, beans and cassava, while annual and/or perennial cotton is the main cash crop. Cashew, castor and melons are also grown. Planted forages include *Opuntia* cactus and elephant grass (*Pennisetum purpureum*). Crops are mainly hand sown but there is some use of animal traction. Perennial cotton is interplanted with maize and beans in its first year but is then a monoculture for the remainder of its 15-year life. The better soils are cultivated every year for long periods, but the poorer ones are abandoned after varying periods and then fallowed for 5–20 years. Overall, 23 per cent of the area is cultivated, varying from 86 per cent on the best soils to zero on poor ones.

Livestock holdings include goats, sheep and cattle, although some farms do not have goats. Small ruminants are important in risk aversion since they can multiply rapidly and tolerate drought. In all 16 different grazing systems can be identified, falling into four major groups, each of which varies in its uses of native vegetation, cropped land and supplementary feed. There are systems in which:

- cattle, sheep and goats remain together throughout the year (Fig 9.4a);
- goats remain in the *caatinga* all the year while other species use crop residues (Fig 9.4b);
- there are normally no goats (Fig 9.4c); and
- farm fences or other infrastructure allow close control of stock (Fig 9.4d).

Crop residues become available in late June/early July after the harvest, the exception being cotton which is harvested somewhat later. Cattle

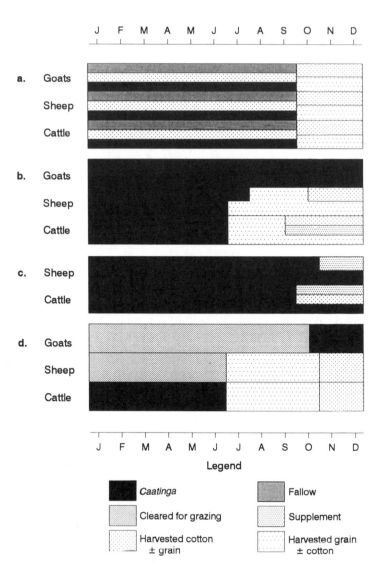

Fig 9.4 *Representative grazing systems in mixed species guilds in north-eastern Brazil (Source: adapted from de Queiroz, J.S., Gutierrez-Aleman, N. and Ponce de León, F.A. 1986. The ecology and management of small ruminant production systems in the sertao of Ceara, in the northeast of Brazil. Agric. Syst. 22: pp. 259–287)*

graze early in the cotton cycle and reduce the need for weeding. Goats receive least attention and often find their feed exclusively in the *caatinga*. Supplements are either purchased or provided from farm resources, including collected crop residues and by-products. Around 85 per cent

Table 9.2 Crop and livestock data from the *sertao* of north-east Brazil

Parameter	All farms			Farms with cattle, sheep and goats			Farms with cattle and sheep[1]		
Number of farms	27			11			10		
Farm size (ha)	312			336			380		
Cropped area (%)	23			20			24		
Livestock numbers	C	S	G	C	S	G	C	S	G
1980	61.0	94.9	47.8	65.0	83.0	64.0	62.0	124.0	0.0
1983	41.1	88.0	74.4	53.0	77.0	92.0	35.0	129.0	29.0
Change (%)	−32.6	−7.3	55.6	−18.5	−7.2	43.8	−43.6	4.3	α
Livestock units[2]									
1980	63.9			67.7			62.8		
1983	40.3			60.8			45.1		
Change (%)	−36.9			−10.2			−28.2		
Stocking rates[3]									
1980	0.19			0.20			0.16		
1983	0.14			0.18			0.12		
Change (%)	−26.3			−10.0			−25.0		

Notes:
1   Farms with no goats in 1980
2   Cattle = 0.79 units, sheep and goats = 0.11 units
3   Livestock units per hectare

Source: adapted from de Queiroz, J.S., Gutierrez-Aleman, N. and Ponce de León, F.A. 1986. The ecology and management of small ruminant production systems in the sertao of Ceara, in the northeast of Brazil. *Agric. Syst.* 22: pp. 259–287

of cattle, 50 per cent of sheep and 30 per cent of goats are supplemented at one time or another. Cattle are the main species culled to maintain seasonal or longer term stocking rates, but cows are retained to produce milk for cash and some small ruminants are also sold for cash.

Sheep are kept in greatest numbers but cattle contribute most to livestock units and to the stocking rate (Table 9.2). Drought in 1980–1983 led farmers to reduce their cattle and switch to goats instead. Farms with goats at the beginning of the drought were able to retain a greater number of livestock units than those without.

Conclusions

There is strong interdependence between crops and livestock. In periods of drought livestock provide a buffer against low crop yields or crop failure, but over the long term neither sub-sector is abandoned in favour of the other. During droughts livestock are more dependent on native vegetation than in better years. Cattle (males, old cows and productive dairy cows) are culled first while goat numbers increase.

10 North African mixed livestock-crop systems

With the exception of the coastal area, the Nile and other river valleys, and the desert oases, livestock are generally the most important component of North Africa's agricultural sector. Within the livestock sub-sector, small ruminants contribute a greater share to numbers (Table 10.1) and to total output than they do elsewhere in the world. There are 59 goats/100 ha in the region, as against 4/100 ha in the world as a whole.

Table 10.1   Livestock populations in the North African region

Country	Livestock species ('000 head)			Goats and sheep as per cent of livestock units
	Goats	Sheep	Cattle	
Algeria	2 004	15 570	1 400	61
Egypt	4 137	4 026	5 532[1]	16
Libya	900	5 600	200	75
Mauritania	3 500	4 000	1 000	48
Morocco	5 807	16 136	3 178	46
Tunisia	1 154	5 846	641	58
Total	17 502	51 178	11 951	40

Note:
1   Includes buffalo

Source: Galal, E.S.E. 1991. Utilization of local genetic resources of small ruminants in North Africa. Paper presented at a Workshop on the Improvement of Small Ruminant Production in North Africa, 27–31 May 1991, Cairo, Egypt

In this region, almost 30 per cent of meat produced is from small ruminants, compared with a world average of less than 6 per cent; in Algeria, Morocco and Tunisia the proportion exceeds 50 per cent. The offtake ratio for sheep of 0.39 (head slaughtered/total numbers) compares favourably with that of the developed countries (0.42). Goats are raised under less favourable conditions than sheep but still achieve a respectable offtake ratio of 0.39 (compared with 0.61 for developed countries). Milk from small ruminants contributes 8 per cent of total milk output in this region, compared with a world average of about 3 per cent, and in both Libya and Mauritania more than 20 per cent of all milk is from small ruminants. Individual milk yields from ewes are higher than anywhere else in the world while from goats the average of 22.2 kg is twice as much as that of the developing world in general.

Goats are well adapted to the desert production systems and the harsh environment. Black Bedouin goats in Sinai, for example, require less feed and can digest poor-quality fodder better than non-native types and, like the camel, can withstand long periods of water deprivation and then drink large amounts quickly to make up the loss.

Large ruminants are also important throughout the region. Cattle are found in all countries as are camels. Buffalo are extremely important in Egypt where they outnumber cattle. They produce meat and milk but their main use is to provide draught power in the oasis systems. Egypt is one of the few areas in the world where one commonly sees the archetypal domestic species associated with water in the same environment as the equally archetypal desert camel (Fig 10.1), which is also a multipurpose animal in this environment.

Fig 10.1   *Camels and buffaloes in Fayum oasis, Egypt*

Major constraints in these areas are the highly fluctuating feed supply, the small and fragmented nature of the enterprises, and the lack of institutional support for small ruminants by bureaucracies and administrations which favour larger-scale commercial development of imported dairy cattle. On the other hand there is a long tradition of small ruminant husbandry for meat and milk production in the region and there are possibilities of good export markets to adjacent regions, particularly in West Asia and the Arab Gulf.

Case study: Goats in the Nile valley and the coastal desert, Egypt

There were about 4 million goats in Egypt in 1988, most being in the regions of Upper Egypt, Sinai and the Red Sea Coast. In Egypt as a whole goats outnumber sheep in the ratio 1.3:1.0, but in the specified regions the ratio is as high as 4.1:1.0. Goats are not differentiated as well as sheep but the Zaraibi, Barki and Wahati are three recognised types, in addition to the nondescript Baladi (Arabic for local).

The Nile valley is home to 84 per cent of the Egyptian goat population. It is an area of intensively farmed land in fragmented holdings, with relatively good supplies of forage and crop residues and by-products. A typical smallholder farmer owns 2 or 3 large ruminants (buffalo and cattle) and up to 5 small ruminants on a farm of 0.2–2.0 ha in size. About 40 per cent of the land area in the winter season is cultivated to *berseem* (*Trifolium* or *Medicago* herbaceous legumes) for stock feed, this being an indication of the importance attached to the livestock enterprise in this area. Goats graze stubbles and may be fed a small amount of supplement in late pregnancy and during the early lactation period. For breeding purposes, males may be individually owned or rented when required, or females may be grazed with the communal flock (tended by a hired herder). Breeding is not seasonal and females are mated and give birth at all times of the year. While in many other systems small ruminants are used to provide regular income and large ruminants are the store of wealth, in the Nile valley it is small ruminants that are the capital account, while daily income is derived from the sale of milk from large ruminants.

Of less importance in the Nile valley are the three other systems.

The *zarrab* system – goats are tethered or penned, takes its name from the Arabic for enclosure and is populated mainly by the Zaraibi goat, which is similar in physical characteristics and production aptitudes to the Sudanese Nubian. Lactation yields of 240 kg in 230 days are cited and litter size is 1.8.

The mobile commercial system – the animal owners may be landless and goats and sheep, in flocks of more than 50 head, graze stubbles in exchange for cash payments or for manure. Owners obtain their income from sales of male animals or of milk or cheese (does have bags over their udders to prevent suckling).

The dairy system – a new intensive development, using imported Anglo-Nubian or French Alpine stock. Milking is by machine and the expensively produced milk and cheese are sold to luxury outlets such as hotels and supermarkets in the larger urban centres.

The coastal area west of Alexandria, about 400 km long and 10–15 km broad, has highly erratic annual rainfall of around 150 mm. Barley is the main annual crop and there are some perennial fruit trees, mostly olive and fig. The transhumant small ruminant production system is rapidly becoming sedentary. Average flock sizes are about 225 head in the range 20–1500 and goats represent about 26 per cent of all small ruminants.

The majority of flocks are looked after by the male owner's spouse(s) or children, while more than a third are under the day-to-day care of hired herders. Animals graze the sparse natural rangelands for 5 winter months and feed on crop residues and aftermaths the remainder of the year. Rangelands provide only 58 per cent of total feed requirements, the remainder being provided by a state-subsidized concentrate allowance of 3 kg/head/month, and by grain, hay and straw. Animals drink rainwater from pools in the winter and spring but obtain water in the hot summer from Roman cisterns – some of these are 2000 years old – and other sources.

Kids are born throughout the year, with peaks in April and November. Kidding intervals are slightly over 12 months (0.96 kiddings/doe/year) and litter sizes average 1.48 young. Kids suckle for 14 weeks and does produce 50 kg of milk in excess of this, which is consumed by the family, either fresh or as curds. Males are sold at 3–4 months at about 16 kg live weight. Fattening for another 3–4 months allows weights of 25–30 kg to be attained. Replacement animals derive from the flock itself.

11 Traditional pastoral systems

In pastoral systems, often known also as range-livestock systems, the principal problem is to match the highly erratic and limited seasonal patterns of primary productivity with the more or less constant feed requirements of the livestock. Various strategies are adopted, including the sophisticated responses of nomadism and transhumance, as well as use of multiple-species animal guilds of different feeding habits and production cycles in what is, in essence, a system without crops.

Traditional pastoral systems are probably more widespread and better documented in Africa than elsewhere but they are found in harsh environments as diverse as the High Andes of South America and the deserts of western Asia. Livestock and their products, including work, provide more than 50 per cent of total household revenue, this being the value of consumed products as well as cash. In Africa, milk from cattle, camels, goats and sheep provides up to 80 per cent of the energy in the human diet, with meat often being of less importance. Blood is drunk by some tribes in eastern Africa. In South America the wool of alpacas and transport by llamas contribute most to household revenue.

Links with the crops sector in pastoral systems are not usually very close, but take a variety of forms. In extreme cases the products of oases are used by both people and animals and include dates as well as fodder crops. Migration sometimes includes a period for grazing crop residues and obtaining water in exchange for manure. Pastoralists' animals provide transport for farmers. Some exchange of pastoral for agricultural production takes place either by barter or through a market system.

Conclusions

Constraints in these systems, other than the obvious ones of water and feed supply, are diverse. Communal land tenure inhibits control of the stocking rate, as reductions in livestock holdings by some members of the group only benefit others. Cultural attitudes are probably more ingrained here than elsewhere and prevent adoption of new or improved technology. Provision of more water, as a political response to pastoral lobbying, often creates more problems than it solves by freeing labour to herd more animals. Markets are far from the areas of production, poorly served by infrastructure and sometimes appear to benefit middlemen more than producers.

Pastoralists are looked down on by administrators and are often last in a long list of development priorities. Yet pastoralism is a system that adds value to vast areas capable of producing little else. Pastoral development has rarely succeeded, technically or economically, but animal production in these zones is usually the only rational way of using them, and efforts to improve it must continue.

Case study: Masai group ranches in southern Kenya

The Kajiado district of Kenya covers about 21 000 km^2. It is just south of the equator (1–3 °S, 36–38 °E) at an altitude of 1000 m to 1500 m. Rainfall is bimodal, a total of 400–600 mm falling mainly in two periods October to November and March to May. There is variable but usually fairly good cover of large thorny shrubs and trees. Rainfall is, of course, highly unpredictable in space and time.

The traditional Masai survival strategy in response to this shifting resource was semi-nomadism. In 1961 even this proved unable to prevent severe losses, particularly of cattle, from drought (Table 11.1). Famine relief maize was provided, some Masai settled and some, in an unprecedented step, even attempted to cultivate maize.

Partly in response to the drought, government initiatives in the 1960s led to the formation of group and individual ranches. This innovation introduced major changes in land tenure, from communal to clearly identified ownership. One result was a stratification of society, with more

Table 11.1 Effects of drought on livestock numbers in a Masai system at Loitokitok, Kenya

Item	Cattle	Sheep	Goats
Per cent of families owning	60	80	90
Group size before drought	84	27	41
Sales	11	2	5
Deaths	25	9	8
Group size after drought	48	16	28
Per cent of original animals after drought	57	59	69

Source: Campbell, D.J. 1978. *Coping with drought in Kenya Masailand: Pastoralists and farmers of the Loitokitok area (Institute for Development Studies Working Paper N° 337)*. University of Nairobi, Kenya

powerful people being able to obtain sole title to land while lower social orders joined group ranches. Dividing the total area of Kajiado district by the number of households would give each family 210 ha of land. Individual ranches managed to appropriate an average of 690 ha each while households on group ranches had only 137 ha.

Group ranches vary enormously in size, however, from less than 9000 ha with about 30 members to as much as 110 000 ha with over 400 members. Ranch size and land availability per person are not related to the number of members, nor even to the potential productivity of the rangeland. Indeed, the individual ranches are usually in the areas of higher potential. One of the aims of the privatisation of the rangelands was to reduce ecological degradation by making pastoralists responsible for their own grazing areas. In this respect group ranches appear to have been more successful than individual ranches as most group ranch members have kept their animals within the confines of their land holdings even in drought years. Most individual ranchers take their animals outside their boundaries every year, indicating that their land is overstocked.

Stratification of wealth is also evident within group ranches and among individual ranches. On both types of ranch the wealthier pastoralists have more cattle per household member than the poorer ones, even though their households are larger in size (Table 11.2). Wealthy families generally own twice as many cattle as goats and sheep, while poorer families own more small ruminants. The third of households comprising

Table 11.2 Household size and livestock holdings on Masai group and individual ranches in Kajiado district, Kenya

Ranch type and Wealth cohort	Household size (Number of people)	Livestock per person	
		Cattle	Sheep + goats
Group (n = 60)			
Above average	17.0	20.5	10.0
Average	15.9	8.1	8.0
Below average	8.5	3.6	7.1
Individual (n = 23)			
Above average	18.6	27.2	13.7
Average	13.6	22.7	13.1
Below average	13.0	11.2	11.0

Source: data from White, J.M. and Meadows, S.J. 1981. *Evaluation of the contribution of group and individual ranches in Kajiado district, Kenya, to economic development and pastoral production strategies.* Ministry of Livestock Development: Nairobi, Kenya

72

Table 11.3 Contribution (per cent) of livestock and other sources to total household income on group and individual ranches in Kenya Masailand

Income component	Type of ranch	
	Group	Individual
Cash income		
Cattle sales	47.8	32.6
Goat and sheep sales	2.5	5.5
Milk sales	2.1	11.5
Other items	4.7	30.9
Subsistence consumption		
Cattle meat	3.5	1.4
Goat and sheep meat	3.5	3.7
Milk	35.9	20.9

Source: data from White, J.M. and Meadows, S.J. 1981. *Evaluation of the contribution of group and individual ranches in Kajiado district, Kenya, to economic development and pastoral production strategies.* Ministry of Livestock Development: Nairobi, Kenya

the wealthy stratum on group ranches own 69 per cent of all cattle and 49 per cent of small ruminants, while the poorest third of households own only 6 per cent of cattle and 15 per cent of goats and sheep. There are similar but less marked variations in ownership on individual ranches.

The Masai are true pastoralists, with more than 95 per cent of the total value of household revenue deriving from the sale or home consumption of livestock products (Table 11.3). One objective of the privatisation of land – to encourage the Masai pastoralist to be more commercially minded – has not been achieved: although about half of total income on group ranches and one third on individual ranches is from sales of cattle the cash value of these sales represents only about 12 per cent of the total value of the herd, while the annual offtake represents only some 8 per cent of herd numbers. Annual expenditure on drugs and vaccines per livestock unit is less than 0.5 per cent of the value of the animal.

Management practices continue to be traditional and aimed at traditional products, of which milk from cattle is by far the most important. Females constitute about 65 per cent of herds, and about 40 per cent of all cattle are cows of breeding age. Calving rates are low (less than 50 per cent), but the aim is to keep sufficient cows so that only about two out of three of those lactating are milked for the household and only about 1 l/cow/day of milk is taken for this purpose. There is no control of the breeding season as it is essential to have a continuous supply of milk for human consumption. A higher percentage figure in total income from

Fig 11.1 *A Masai goat with a leather apron to help with control of breeding*

milk sales on individual ranches indicates some attempt at commercial production, but income from other sources, mainly the sale of labour, indicates that these ranches are not entirely viable.

There is some control of breeding in both goats and sheep, this being achieved by the use of a leather apron attached to the buck (Fig 11.1) or the ram. The control is said to be aimed not at manipulating the season of breeding but at allowing hand-mating to be managed by the owner. This practice does, however, lead to advanced ages at first parturition – about 550 days for both species – and long intervals of about 350–360 days between successive parturitions. Litter sizes of about 1.20 in goats and 1.05 in sheep give annual reproductive rates of about one or slightly more than 1 young/ breeding female/year. The principal products of the small ruminant component of the species mix are meat and fat for home consumption. Males surplus to breeding are, therefore, castrated and kept to fairly advanced ages; resultant flock structures have rather fewer females (65 per cent of total numbers) than is normal in African small ruminant flocks and considerably more mature castrates (10–12 per cent) than found elsewhere (except in societies where wool or hair is a principal product).

Conclusions

The Masai occasionally cultivate, and now consume, considerable quantities of maize. There is, however, little integration of livestock with crops and little direct exchange of livestock for agricultural produce with neighbouring cultivating tribes. Any improvements in output in this

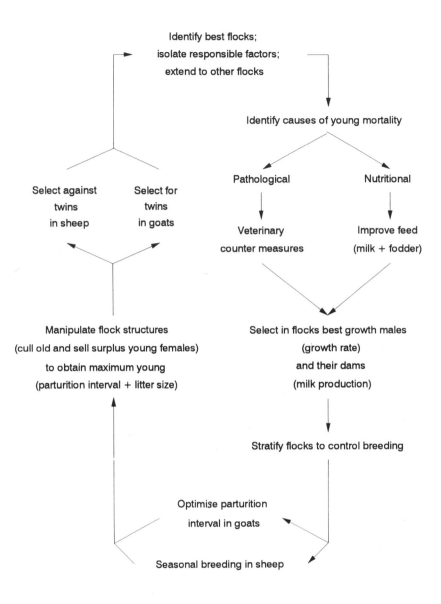

Fig 11.2 *Potential improvement pathways for traditionally managed small ruminant flocks on Masai group ranches in Kenya (Source: Wilson, R.T., Peacock, C.P. and Sayers, A.R. 1985. Pre-weaning mortality and productivity indices for goats and sheep on a Masai group ranch in south-central Kenya. Anim. Prod. 41: pp. 201–206)*

system will, therefore, need to concentrate on the animal component. Veterinary and nutritional interventions may be easier to implement in the first place with goats and sheep (Fig 11.2).

Case study: Touareg desert pastures in the Aïr region, Niger

The Aïr region of northern Niger is typical sand desert on the southern fringe of the Sahara and is centred on 17 °N, 7 °W. Annual rainfall is low (150 mm) and highly erratic. Daytime temperatures can soar to more than 50 °C every day for several months. At night the temperature falls below freezing from November to February. Diurnal variations in temperature of almost 40 °C are common and add to the stress imposed on people and animals. There is very sparse woody vegetation of low, thorny shrubs, which tends to be thicker in small favoured areas, such as wadi beds and where water collects in depressions or at the foot of rocky screes. Several species of *Acacia* (including *A. tortilis* and *A. nilotica* on the better sites) are dominant, but there are other genera including *Boscia* and the desert date (*Balanites aegyptiaca*) as well as *Ziziphus spina-christi*, this last providing edible fruits for man as well as good-quality high-protein browse for camels and goats. Ground cover is mainly sparse ephemeral grasses (*Stipa*, *Agrostis* and *Aristida* spp.), with some herbs (Leguminosae or Chenopodiaceae), but the perennial grass *Panicum turgidum* provides valuable green feed over relatively extended periods of the annual cycle.

The system is totally pastoral with almost all income deriving from livestock – including earnings from transport by camels and donkeys of salt to the south and of agricultural and other items to the north on the return journey – and some from sale of labour either as house guards in Nigeria and elsewhere or to the uranium mines farther north in Niger. Livestock feed is usually very limited in supply but the scarcity of water and the depth from which it has to be drawn using human and animal

Fig 11.3   *A deep hand-dug well in Niger that uses human and animal power for drawing water*

power (Fig 11.3) are instrumental in keeping stocking rates at a low level. During some favourable periods the fleshy stems and leaves of Chenopodiaceae contain sufficient liquid for livestock to be independent of free water for several days or even weeks.

Camels are the dominant domestic animal, followed by sheep and goats. There are very few cattle. Some horses are kept but every family has one or more donkeys which are used to lift water from wells and transport it and other burdens to the highly mobile camps. Camels are the main source of milk, consumed by their owners, and are also used to transport the tent and household goods as well as in commercial transport of salt (Fig 11.4). Goats and camels both produce hair which is mainly used to manufacture the tent. Goats and sheep also provide milk, the sheep's milk being used mainly to manufacture a hard cheese which is stored for use in leaner times.

The average household herd of camels is just under 20 head, but 20 per cent of households own 5 or less. The 42 per cent of households owning 20 or more camels have about 75 per cent of all camels. Female camels account for 59.6 per cent of the herd, with about 34 per cent of the total number of animals being females over 5 years old. The relatively large proportion of males reflects their economic role as transport animals. The breeding period is markedly seasonal, related to the short flush of good nutrition associated with the rains. Camels give birth the first time at 5.0 ± 1.69 years although some do not have their first calf until 11 years. The calving interval is 26.2 ± 10.56 months but is longer in younger than in older females. Only 42 per cent of females of breeding age give birth each year and this low rate, associated with late ages at first parturition and relatively early ages at culling or death, gives rise to a

Fig 11.4   *A camel train transporting salt in Niger*

lifetime production of young of about 2.7 per female.

Goat flocks average just under 60 head and have a very high proportion of females (86 per cent, 67 per cent of which are of breeding age). This indicates a very early offtake of males, probably aimed at reducing the stocking rate. Only 3.8 per cent of the total flock consists of males over 6 months old. Age at first parturition is 15–18 months, kidding interval about 10 months and litter size about 1.15. A fairly high early mortality rate of about 30 per cent of animals before weaning means that the offtake rate, almost all of which is for home consumption, is 25–28 per cent.

As in all Muslim societies, sheep are important to the Touareg and flock sizes are larger than those of goats, averaging 103 head. Females constitute 82 per cent of the flock (64 per cent of breeding age) but, unlike goats, a few males are allowed to grow on for sacrifice at the main Islamic festivals. These are slaughtered at about 2 years at a weight of 55–60 kg. Some breeding control is practised, as is common in many Muslim communities in northern Africa and the Near East. First lambing in sheep is delayed somewhat in comparison with goats and takes place at 18–20 months, with subsequent lambing intervals being of about 12 months. Litter size is about 1.03. Ewes produce only about 4 young in their life compared with 7 or 8 from goats. Offtake is about 22–25 per cent.

Conclusions

There is little interaction with agriculture in this desert pastoral society. On some very small areas a few metres square, crops may be grown around water holes, in particular the Cucurbitaceae, which are used as gourds and calabashes. Camels are sometimes hired out to the Hausa, an agro-pastoral tribe inhabiting the desert fringe, to transport the crop harvest, while the donkey herd provides a surplus of males for sale to these and other cultivating peoples.

Feed availability, or rather its lack, might be considered a constraint in this system, but it is water which really restricts stock numbers. Making more water available might not be feasible in this area, but even if it were it could perhaps paradoxically destroy the system, which at present appears to be reasonably in balance with resources and sustainable in the long term.

Case study: Karakul pelt production in Botswana

Pelt producing sheep probably originated in the Near East (Syria, Jordan and western Mesopotamia) and Karakul flocks were established about 1200 years ago in Bokhara and China. Karakuls were imported to southern Africa in 1907 from Germany, and to south-west Botswana in 1953.

Fig 11.5   *Karakul lambs of varying pelt types in Botswana*

Numbers had increased to about 30 000 on 200 farms by 1978, but by 1987 had declined to about 14 000 in 80 flocks.

The sheep thrive best in arid to hyper-arid areas. In south-west Botswana rainfall is less than 200 mm per year; maximum temperature in January averages 35.8 °C and minimum temperature in July averages 0.9 °C; there are 35 frost nights/year. The region's carrying capacity is estimated at 27 ha/TLU. Its low vegetative cover consists mainly of grass species such as *Stipagrostis* and *Aristida,* while shrubs include *Acacia, Boscia* and *Rhizogum trichotomum.* The fruits of *Citrullus lanatus, C. naudinianus* and *Cucumis africanus* are important food and water sources in the winter.

In 1991 there were 11 'commercial' fenced farms (although these were effectively managed traditionally) averaging 7100 ha in area with a mean flock size of 550 animals. Flock structures are related to pelt production, for which animals must be slaughtered immediately after birth, and they are, therefore, 95 per cent or more female.

The annual number of lambings is 1.39 and litter size is very low, with twin births occurring in less than 10 out of 1000 births. In flocks with predominantly Karakul breeding 43 per cent of lambs are slaughtered for pelt production and 57 per cent are reared. This constrasts with more efficient farms in South Africa and Namibia, where only 17–20 per cent of lambs are reared. More lambs are slaughtered for pelt production in dry years, and major losses may have induced owners to increase replacement rates.

The coat is of coarse wool in the adult (4488 kg of wool was sold to a co-operative by 171 farmers in 1985) and it is the skin of the new born lamb, which varies in texture (Fig 11.5), that is the pelt of commerce. Lambs used for pelt production must be slaughtered the day after birth, otherwise the characteristic curls and patterns disappear. Slaughtering and skinning is done by knife and by hand. Tissue and fat are removed with a knife and blood and dirt washed out with cold water. The wet pelt is spread, without fixing, on a frame covered with jute and dries in this form in the air. Most pelts are shipped to London for classification according to a standard system. The prices of pelts are related to colour, with grey pelts better priced than black or chequered ones; pelt size, which depends on litter size and the nutrition and age of the ewe; curl type, with shallower types achieving better prices; hair length and curl size, with short hair or small curls preferred to the overgrown hair associated with years of good nutrition; hair quality, which is determined by lustre and texture; and, lastly, hair pattern.

The prices fetched by pelts from Botswana are lower than the average for southern Africa, probably because of small pelt size and poor quality. Small pelt size is caused by poor ewe nutrition. Pelt quality is related mainly to colour. Botswana has a high proportion of pied pelts, reflecting the high proportion of crossbred animals in the country's flocks.

Pelt production on Botswana farms averages 74 annually, with a total income of £710. Farms that are fenced do not achieve higher incomes than unfenced ones in the same area. Average prices and total income are higher in areas with lower rainfall. The proportion of Karakul ewes in the flock affects the number of pelts produced, but not the average price obtained.

Conclusions

Constraints in this system could be overcome by more government support (as in South Africa and Namibia), by genetic improvement of the sheep and by emphasising the production of high-value black pelts. Improvements in pelt treatment and the provision of training in pelt selection for farmers would also help. The proper use of sales records could improve management practices.

Case study: The Latin American savanna system

The savanna region covers much of central South America, where the word originated. Rainfall is high (1200–2400 mm/year) but erratic and falls in a period of 6–8 months. Soils, however, are highly weathered, have poor water holding capacity and are very acid. Crop production is, therefore, risky. Interest in agriculture is further depressed by the land tenure system, in which absentee landlords predominate and the farms, which may be as large as 100 ha, are managed by hired labour. The population density is low.

Cattle grazing for meat production is the principal form of land use.

Output per hectare is low because of the poor quality of the native vegetation and the small amount of feed available during the dry season. Cattle reproduction rates are poor and weight gains are very low.

There is little to no integration of crops with livestock, as hired labourers grow minor crops for their own use but are obviously not interested in providing feed for the employers' animals. A further problem is poor access to markets.

Conclusions

Improvements in this system are likely to be costly and time-consuming. There is a need to improve animal nutrition by the introduction or breeding of fodder species adapted to acid and infertile soils. The introduction of improved rice-pasture rotations in recent years has shown some promise, bringing gains in soil fertility and sustainability of production, as well as improved profitability. The introduction of small ruminants would diversify the production process, reduce risk and allow a more even cash flow. The use of animal manure could help to increase crop production, particularly where night holding pens have been located. Better animal productivity could also be achieved if younger animals were shipped out for finishing elsewhere, but this would also require more efficient marketing channels and a greatly improved transport infrastructure.

Case study: South American camelids in the high Andes

In the very high altitude areas of Peru and Bolivia there are few alternatives to a precarious pastoral existence because of the constraints imposed by climate and ecology. In Bolivia, llamas and alpaca annually produce about 550 000 skins, 1000 t of wool and 9000 t of meat, and they are the principal source of income of more than 200 000 people. In Peru, more than 3500 t of fibre and 14 000 t of meat, as well as skins and transport services, support 200 000 families.

In the area of Peru bounded by 14 and 15 °S and 70 and 72 °W the altitude varies from 3900 m to more than 5000 m. Alpaca are the principal livestock at the higher altitudes (Table 11.4) and between 68 per cent and 85 per cent of household income derives from their products. Precipitation includes rain, hail and snow (and dew) but the total amount is low (<600 mm) and erratic. The fragile ecology supports a discontinuous vegetation, classed into various altitudinal zones from humid sub-Andean sub-tropical to cold-temperate Andean desert. Shrubby species include *Clusia*, *Eugenia*, *Ocotea*, *Myrica* and *Solanum*. The field layer has both perennial herbs and grasses, with *Calamagrotis*, *Festuca*, *Stipa* and *Carex* often being dominant or co-dominant although there are many other

Table 11.4 Proportions of cattle, sheep and camelids at varying altitudes in a Peruvian Andean pastoral system

Altitude (metres)	Total animals	Species (per cent of all animals)		
		Cattle	Sheep	Camelids
<4000	15 772	10	89	1
4000–4300	37 598	7	76	17
>4300	88 050	3	31	66

Source: Leyva, V. 1989. Sistemas de producción de alpacas. In: *Simposio producción de alpacas y llamas (XII Reunion Científica Anual de la Asociación Peruana de Producción Animal)*. Universidad Nacional Mayor de San Marcos: Lima, Peru: pp. 157–174

temperate and alpine genera, including *Bromus, Alchemilla, Agrostis, Poa, Viola, Gentiana* and *Plantago*.

Flock sizes of alpaca vary from small to very large, but 72 per cent of flocks are in the range 100–700 head. Above 4300 m most flocks in the hands of small producers range from 150 to 300. Crop production is limited to small areas of 400–800 m², and a cow provides some milk, but as much as 82 per cent of income is from alpaca wool. Llama are used to transport this product to market, typically carrying loads of 25–35 kg for up to 40 km. The poor quality wool from this species is used to make the saddle bags that are used to contain the higher quality product of the alpaca.

The birth rate in alpacas is about 50 per cent and is slightly higher on small farms than on larger units. The young weigh about 7 kg at birth, while adults attain 55–65 kg. Mortality before weaning is normally in the region of 15–20 per cent, but may rise to 35 per cent; in mature stock it is about 4 per cent/year. The low reproductive rate and high mortality result in offtakes of about 10 per cent (of which half is home consumption), although the better producers achieve twice this. Fibre yields are 1.7 kg in first-year animals and 2.5 kg in older animals.

Conclusions

There is very little integration with agriculture here and farmers glean a meagre living in a very difficult environment. The climate is a major constraint, about which little can be done. Additional constraints are the poor quality of the overgrazed native pastures which are used continuously without any rest or rotation; the system of land tenure, which is communal; the excessive use of the sparse woody cover as fuel; and the distance from markets, the lack of roads and other rural infrastructure.

Some of these additional constraints can be alleviated, provided governments are committed to improving the lives of their Andean populations. Improved pastures, provided for only a short period during pregnancy, have led to increased rates of birth by alpaca. Extension advice and the provision of drugs have helped to reduce mortality in some trial flocks. The formation of co-operatives to gather, clean and grade wool would render the individual producer less susceptible to exploitation by middlemen.

12 Modern pastoral systems

Modern pastoralism is usually similar to its traditional counterparts in the extensive use of land but differs more or less radically in livestock functions. For example: Namibia, contained 4205 'commercial' ranches in 1991; sheep ranches averaged 11 600 ha in size and carried stock at a rate of about 2.5 ha/TLU, while cattle ranches averaged 6600 ha and were stocked at 7.3 ha/TLU. Cattle contributed about 60 per cent of gross income on all Namibian ranches, small ruminant meat and Karakul pelts about 25 per cent, with the balance from game farming and crops. In Lesotho a modern pastoral system is being developed based on co-operative groups of small-scale owners producing wool and mohair as major products. This system draws on experience and genetic resources from large operations in South Africa and Zimbabwe.

Modern systems should in theory also differ in management capability and in productivity, but this is not always the case. Ranches usually specialise in one product:

- mature beef (the most common specialisation);
- dairy products;
- sheep and/or goat production for meat and wool;
- cow-calf operations (modern pastoralism);
- stud breeding options in modern pastoralism; or
- sport hunting (in some areas is still, or again, becoming a vogue).

In modern systems livestock are raised to produce cash and not for subsistence. In addition to its management and production objectives, ranching differs from traditional pastoralism in supporting fewer people on the land, in always being sedentary, in land tenure (which is individual although not necessarily private), and in the options for intensifying water and feed supplies. As a result of these differences there is usually some long-term intention to adjust stocking rates to carrying capacity, indicating an acceptance of responsibility for sustainable production. There may also be attempts to diversify the production base and to ensure sustainability by, for example, incorporating wildlife into the system.

Ranching systems are the major form of land use over large parts of Latin America and tropical Australia, and are important in some parts of Africa. They are usually associated, as are traditional pastoral systems, with arid to semi-arid areas and there is normally little or no integration of livestock with crops. Modern pastoral systems may also be found in some wetter areas, however, where distance from markets or other factors have prevented the development of crop production. While remaining extensive, the ranches usually evolve with time towards more intensive systems through the installation of water points, the erection of fences, the building of handling yards and dips or spray races, and the cultivation of forages to alleviate fluctuations in seasonal feed supply.

Case study: Parastatal ranches in Tanzania

The Tanzanian National Agricultural Company (NAC) was a subsidiary of the giant parastatal National Development Corporation of Tanzania. The NAC was the successor to the Tanganyika Agricultural Corporation, formerly the Overseas Food Corporation – the ill-fated Groundnut Scheme. In the mid-1960s the company owned six ranches, two of which – Kongwa and Nachingwea in the Central and Southern Regions respectively – were former groundnut properties. Two other ranches at Mkata, near Morogoro, and at Ruvu, inland from Dar es Salaam, were originally run by the country's Veterinary Department. Kitengule, near Bukoba in the West Lake Region, was acquired in early 1965 and was the only ranch of the six which was started by the Corporation purely as a ranch. The ranch at West Kilimanjaro was an amalgamation of three small ranches, purchased from settler owners and then run as one unit. Additional ranches were set up later in the 1960s.

Some ranches moved away from extensive cattle raising for beef to mixed meat/milk production (dairy ranching). Some better sections of some ranches (with good quality soils or higher rainfall) were switched to intensive dairy or even crop production. Some ranches had sheep and one had an intensive pig enterprise. The World Bank provided long-term loans to finance some of these operations and changes. The pure ranching operations attempted to model themselves on Australian or the better of the Kenyan ranching systems (Fig 12.1). Cattle numbers increased from about 40 000 to about 50 000 from 1966 to 1968 and were expected to rise to 70 000–80 000 in the mid-1970s.

Management objectives, as well as management ability, varied greatly. The introduction of better cost accounting and the keeping of physical records often led to a general improvement in performance in the short run, but matters usually deteriorated again in the longer term, partly through socialist policies of centralised control, rapid turnover of management staff, and some staff dishonesty.

Fig 12.1   *Boran cattle in a modern pastoral system on the Athi Plains near Nairobi, Kenya*

Animal performance fluctuated widely among ranches and years. Ages at first calving varied from 2.5 years to 4.0 years depending on ranch situation, ranch policy and breed (ranches with exotic crossbreds tended to be earlier). At West Kilimanjaro heifers mated for the first time at 2.5 years showed 98 per cent conception rates and the 2 per cent of failures were culled without further consideration. Calving rates rarely reached the 87 per cent (13.8 months interval) typical of the Kenyan ranches and were usually 75 per cent (16.0 month interval) or less. Mortality rates to weaning were generally in the 5–10 per cent range and annual adult mortality 3–5 per cent. Weaning weights were very variable, from 120 kg on ranches with predominantly local Tanzania Shorthorned Zebu stock to 200 kg on the two stud ranches at Kongwa and West Kilimanjaro. Cattle on the latter ranch were considered highly desirable by the surrounding traditional Masai pastoralists, who were wont periodically to make off with 50 or 100 head, leading to a high percentage of livestock losses in total ranch costs.

Kitengulc ranch, at an early stage of development, spent relatively little directly on livestock but had heavy transport costs for construction of dips and fences. Income in the early years was mainly from births and the rapid sale of steers bought in for fattening. Nachingwea and Kongwa (the old Groundnut Scheme ranches) spent relatively little on direct livestock operations but had high transport charges and water overheads. Stock losses at Kongwa were low thanks to experienced management and a semi-arid environment, but were very high at Nachingwea (where cattle had been imported to an artificial ranch to supply beef to the military) because of inexperienced management, East Coast Fever and trypanosomiasis.

Mkata and Ruvu spent more directly on the livestock enterprise than other ranches, with heavy dipping charges to control ticks and drugs charges for trypanosome control. Both were new ranches with relatively few vehicles and tractors, and low water costs owing to an abundance of surface water. Livestock losses were still costly on these ranches, where most income derived from livestock sales, particularly on Ruvu which was a fattening and not a breeding ranch.

At West Kilimanjaro direct livestock costs were about average for the group as were vehicle operating and water costs. Vehicle costs could have been considerably higher, as the nature of the terrain necessitated expensive 4-wheel drive vehicles (most other ranches used conventional pick-up trucks), but were kept down by the use of horses for some operations and donkeys for supplying herds with salt and other items.

Managers' salaries varied among ranches, mainly according to whether expatriate or local staff were employed. Overheads on all ranches appeared to be a heavy burden in relation to other costs.

Conclusions

Modern pastoral systems have little connection with agriculture unless they grow forage or other feed crops and unless they buy agricultural products for feeding to animals. Constraints appear to be similar worldwide: operations are far removed from markets, costs escalate in terms of inputs and labour but returns remain low, often because there are government controls on the prices paid for live animals or the retail price of meat. The most profitable enterprises are those which reduce overheads to a minimum, operate on high animal to labour ratios, and can find a profitable sub-sector of the market such as the sale of bulls for stud or of cows either for breeding more beef stock or especially as foundation dairy animals.

Case study: Game production

The rationale for game production or wildlife harvesting is its value as an alternative, sustainable land use system. The incorporation of multi-species guilds in a land use plan should allow more even use of the total feed resources and an increase in the total stocking rate in terms of biomass carried. Meat from controlled hunting is a major product, but sport hunting for trophies can also be a producer of very high incomes. Game harvesting still has important economic and social implications in some traditional societies.

Because of the large biomass of wild animals, Africa is the centre of game production in the tropics. Within Africa game production is concentrated in Kenya, Zimbabwe and South Africa, especially for meat.

Possibilities exist, and are often exploited, for sport hunting in most countries of the continent.

The major species exploited for meat belong to the Bovinae, Tragelaphini and Antelopini tribes of the Bovidae. Amongst the larger animals are buffalo (*Syncerus caffer*), eland (*Taurotragus oryx*), the two oryxes (*Oryx oryx* and *O. gazella*), impala (*Aepyceros melampus*) (Fig 12.2), hartebeest (*Alcelaphus* spp.), and wildebeest (*Connochaetes* spp.) and possibly one Suidae, the hippopotamus (*Hippopotamus amphibius*). Smaller species include Grant's and Thomson's gazelles (*Gazella granti* and *G. thomsonii*), springbok (*Antidorcas marsupialis*), and some species of duiker (*Sylvicapra* spp.). Zebra (*Equus* spp.) are also exploited for meat. Most of these animals are also capable of producing trophies (horns and skins) or other products for manufacture for the curio or tourist trades.

The ostrich (*Struthio camelus*) (Fig 12.3) is farmed in southern Africa for meat, skins, feathers and eggs. Since the opening up of the USA to imports of captive or ranched birds and products in 1990 there has been a new boom in this industry, particularly for eggs for hatching. Many smaller bird species, such as ducks and geese, guinea fowl and other Phasianidae, bustards and pigeons, are also hunted commercially.

Sport hunting, mainly aimed nowadays at a very specialised clientele, and restricted to a few countries that have convinced the international conservation lobby that they can manage their wildlife sustainably, can provide a huge income at infrequent intervals. It is essentially limited to the main predators – lion (*Panthera leo*), leopard (*P. pardus*) and cheetah (*Acinonyx jubatus*) (Fig 12.4) – and some prestige herbivores such as buffalo, elephant (*Loxodonta africana*), and the black rhinoceros (*Diceros bicornis*). Culling or game control operations are often provided as justifications for this type of operation.

At its simplest, game production involves the periodic or continuous cropping of large populations of wild animals, principally herbivores, in their natural state. This may be justified as culling to prevent overgrazing, protect crops or clear out potential disease reservoirs (e.g. of trypanosomiasis). Specific classes of stock may be hunted or a decision taken to eliminate whole social groups (herds or family units) within a larger population. Such a management system is usually under national or regional government control, requires (or at any rate usually receives) little in the way of inputs, and can generate considerable income.

Sport hunting is at a slightly more sophisticated level. Hunting licences or permits for individual animals are issued by the responsible government department to a client, but the organisation of safaris is usually farmed out to professional hunters. These provide a bespoke service, including aeroplane tickets, hotel reservations in the capital, customs clearance of arms and ammunition, transport to the hunting site (to which the target

Fig 12.2   *A female impala* (Aepyceros melampus) *ready for flight*

Fig. 12.3   Ostriches on a farm in the Republic of South Africa

Fig 12.4   *A cheetah* (Acinonyx jubatus) *stalking the impala in Fig 12.2*

animal may have been lured with bait), luxurious tented accommodation, skinning and mounting of trophies, and transport of clients and trophies back to the home country.

There is currently a move towards more intensive utilisation of wildlife, particularly in southern Africa and, to a lesser extent, in Kenya. The justification, in addition to the national land use argument, is that game must have an economic as well as an aesthetic function. The position is controversial in the extreme: it is supported by some conservation organisations and opposed by others. Part of the controversy arises from the fact that, for example, elephant tusks or rhino horn are banned on the world market if taken in the wild or poached, but can be sold on a quota system if obtained legally. There is very little hope, following sale on the world market, that legal can be distinguished from illegal origin.

Intensification of game production for meat usually implies devolving ownership, from government or a traditional rights group, to an individual. That individual is then in a position to invest in infrastructure such as fencing, possibly improved water supplies, and perhaps an abattoir and a small factory for the manufacture of curios. Animals are not ranched as such, being simply shot or rounded up for slaughter. A few trophy licences may also be granted.

One such operation in Kenya called for a reduction in the stocking rate of domestic ruminants from a biomass of 86 kg/ha to 44 kg/ha and an increase in game biomass from 12 kg/ha to 16 kg/ha. Paradoxically, total biomass was reduced from 98 kg/ha to 61 kg/ha in this intensified system, justified on the grounds that game meat had higher unit value than beef. As game animals were not herded or provided with dipping and veterinary care, variable costs were reduced. Males were harvested in the early stages to provide a sex ratio of 1:10, at which level females were also harvested. Meat was inspected and rated according to government standards used for domestic animals. The best cuts were sold fresh, while poorer cuts were turned into sausages, smoked meat, *biltong* and pet food. Average dressing percentages in 1984 were 54, 54, 53 and 54 per cent of live weight for Thomson's gazelle, Grant's gazelle, Coke's hartebeest and wildebeest respectively. Total annual meat production on the cattle/game ranch was about 11 kg/ha in 1981–1984 compared with just over 8 kg/ha on adjacent cattle ranches. Economic calculations showed that the wildlife operation could expect to achieve about twice the gross income, in the initial phase of operations, than a ranch with cattle only, and about ten times the net income at maturity (Fig 12.5).

Conclusions

Constraints in this system are numerous and varied. Initial capital investment in game-proof fencing is very high. Predation by wild animals

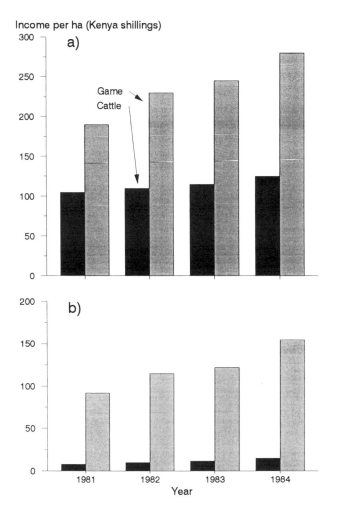

Fig 12.5 *A comparison of returns to cattle and cattle/game production in terms of (a) gross and (b) net income in Kenya (Source: Hopcraft, D. 1988. The ecological and economic validity of wildlife in the semi-arid tropics. In: Gosh, P.K. and Prakash, I. (eds),* Ecophysiology of desert vertebrates. *Scientific Publishers: Jodpur, India: pp. 373–392)*

and poaching by people can be major problems. Management skills need to be of a high order and veterinary controls must often be strict to prevent cross-infection to nearby domestic animals. In some countries marketing is restricted by legislation to prevent illegal hunting. The rewards, however, can be high. The exotic nature of the product attracts high prices, while treatment such as smoking or pickling can further enhance income. Much game meat also has low calorific value and is low in cholesterol, making it suitable for the health food market. In the early stages of development the prices obtained from the sale of breeding stock can be very high. The system can contribute to sustainable production and the biological diversity of dry lands, broadening the resource base and helping to reduce risks for the operator.

Case study: Co-operative wool and mohair production in Lesotho

The Merino sheep is native to Spain. Its major strongholds as a wool breed are Australia (where most research has been done) and Argentina, and as a mutton breed in Germany and some other countries. The Angora goat probably originated in the Himalayas but its modern development dates from the middle of the sixteenth century in the Angora region of Turkey. Mohair production was a Turkish monopoly until the early nineteenth century.

There are large populations of Merinos in South Africa, in Lesotho, in Zimbabwe (where they are equivalent to about 13 per cent of the commercial flock) and in Kenya. Southern Africa also has a relatively large population of Angora goats, and is now the world's main mohair producing area. The first Angora importation into South Africa was of 12 bucks (rendered sterile by the Turks) and one female in 1838. The female gave birth to a male kid and this became the foundation of the South African national flock.

Merino sheep were first introduced to Lesotho in the late nineteenth century. The administration imported 85 rams in 1908 and 286 in 1910. A further 1799 rams and 707 ewes were imported from South Africa in 1986, when numbers in Lesotho were estimated at 1.5 million. Most

Fig 12.6   *An Angora buck imported from South Africa in a Lesotho co-operative flock*

Merino sheep are owned by small farmers. These were organised in producer co-operatives that had 1877 members in 1982 and 4234 in 1986. It is probable that Lesotho Angoras arrived as thefts or purchases by labourers returning from farms in South Africa. In 1908 the Lesotho administration imported 35 bucks and a further 140 were imported in 1910. No stud is established in Lesotho and 275 bucks were imported from South Africa in 1986 (Fig 12.6). The Angora goat population was estimated at 1.0 million in Lesotho in 1986 and it is so important to the economy that it is depicted on a coin. About 30 per cent of all households now own sheep and/or goats. Flock sizes increase with the age of the household head, owners over 60 years old having around 49 sheep, while those in the 21–40 years bracket have only 41. The proportion of livestock (animal sales plus fibre) to total income also increases with the age of the owner but is about 25 per cent overall. Only 12 per cent of flocks are owned or managed by women whose flocks are small.

Merino sheep in Lesotho yield 2.2–2.5 kg/year of wool, according to records of co-operatives which shear, sort and sell the commodity (Fig 12.7). Total wool yield in Lesotho increased from about 2400 t in 1977/1978 to 3400 t in 1986/1987 while its value rose sixfold.

Mohair yields were 0.82 kg/head in Lesotho in 1976 and 0.80 kg/head in 1986. The mohair produced in 1977/1978 amounted to 507 t; production rose to 788 t some 8 years later (Fig 12.8). In contrast, first-clip kids yield about 1.0 kg at six months in Kenya and mature females about 3.0 kg/year in two clips, while in South Africa the average yield was 4.26 kg in 1984. The fibre is very fine with an average diameter of 27–32 μm. Kemp constitutes about 44 per cent of fibres at birth but this is reduced to 7 per cent at 3 months. Kid mohair should be baled separately from adult hair and carries a premium of about 25–30 per cent over

Fig 12.7   *Machine shearing of Merino sheep in a producer co-operative in Lesotho*

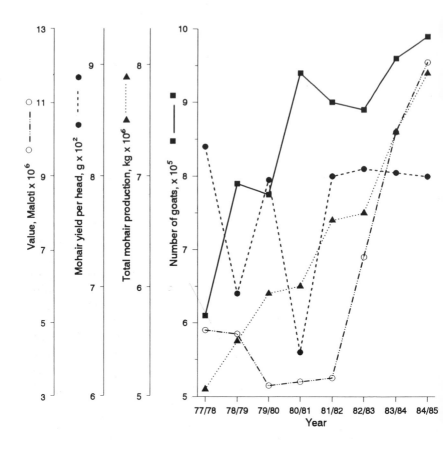

Fig 12.8   *Biological and economic parameters of Mohair production in Lesotho (Source: adapted from Makhooane, L. 1987. Goat and sheep production in Lesotho. Small Rum. Camel Group Newsl. 9: pp. 3–5)*

adult hair. Mohair is used mainly for fine suitings and knitting yarns but also in space suits, as it is radiation resistant.

Conclusions

Wool and mohair production in Lesotho is developing from a traditional to a modern system of production. The two commodities now account for more than 20 per cent of the value of agricultural output. Wool and mohair also comprise over 43 per cent of the value of the country's exports. They are the largest single source of on-farm income for farmers and account for 75 per cent of all livestock earnings. Sheep and goats for fibre production are an important form of investment for migrant labourers and a major repository of rural wealth.

Over most of the country there is little integration of sheep and goats with crop production. Fibre yields in Lesotho are low compared with those obtained elsewhere and sale prices also compare unfavourably with neighbouring countries. Among the reasons are overgrazing, poor nutrition, and the penning of animals at night which leads to short grazing times and soiling of the fibre by dung. It is also probable that Lesotho livestock are genetically inferior to those in South Africa. Some marginal areas are used for fibre production, which further depresses overall national yields. The establishment of co-operatives to organise, to train and to extend production techniques to farmers is one component of a programme which should lead to greater efficiency.

13 Landless and urban systems

Many people who do not own land, other than perhaps the very small plot on which they live, nevertheless own productive domestic animals. Landless livestock production systems are found in rural areas all over Asia, while urban systems are common everywhere in the developing world. Such systems are seldom influenced by climate and ecology. This chapter describes small-scale systems with low input and output. Larger scale intensive systems with small requirements for land are dealt with in chapter 15.

- Poultry and pigs are the species which lend themselves best to these systems. Poultry covers several species, including fowl, guinea fowl, ducks and pigeons.
- Goats, sheep and the larger ruminants may also be found.
- Milk cattle, in particular, appear to be gaining in importance as the urban demand for milk rises.
- Equines and other transport animals are also important in some urban systems, both to provide transport and to carry in feed from the countryside for themselves and other species.

In rural landless systems much animal feed is gleaned from roadside verges and similar unexploited spots. In urban systems the major feed source, particularly for pigs and poultry, is household waste, which is scavenged by the animals not only in the household of the owner but also on communal middens (Fig 13.1). Where dairy cattle are found in urban systems there is normally insufficient feed available for them to produce satisfactory levels of milk and some degree of intensification takes place through the purchase of concentrate feeds or of hay and crop residues brought in from the urban hinterland – a drain on resources which the rural ecosystem (as opposed to the economic system) can usually ill afford.

Conclusions

Production is usually geared to home consumption, but there is always the possibility of raising income from the sale of small surpluses. Early success in this kind of enterprise may lead to spontaneous intensification. More co-ordinated efforts to encourage such a process could be made by local authorities in attempts to alleviate what are often chronic shortages of milk, meat and eggs in urban areas. Intensification only rarely benefits producers, who find themselves progressively less rewarded for both their labour and their investment (Table 13.1).

Table 13.1 Stratification and production economics of landless poultry production in Kenya

| Parameter | Production system | | | |
	Traditional subsistence	Semi-commercial dual purpose	Commercial egg production	Commercial broiler production
Number of birds	10	20	200	2000
Output per person-day				
Eggs (number)	60	145	431	–
Meat (kg)	9	3	5	168
Output per unit cash				
Eggs (number)	1.60	2.68	9.86	–
Meat (kg)	0.24	0.05	0.01	0.05
Gross margin (cash units)				
Per person-day	74	64	25	–186
Per cash unit	1.97	1.19	0.06	–0.06

Source: adapted from Smith, C. 1980. *The economics of small scale poultry production in Kenya.* National Poultry Development Programme: Nairobi, Kenya

Fig 13.1 *Urban pigs scavenging a public midden in Benin, West Africa*

Case study: Multi-species poultry in West Africa

It is unusual to own only one species of poultry in most West African countries. All possible combinations exist among fowl, guinea fowl, ducks (usually Muscovy) and pigeons. In Cameroon, 74 per cent of families own an average of 5.2 birds and flock sizes increase from 4.1 in houses of 3–5 persons to 13.6 in houses of 16 or more people. Pigs are usually owned in conjunction with poultry, but while only 24 per cent of pigs are owned by women and 2 per cent by children, 57 per cent and 9 per cent of poultry are owned by these two groups. In Côte d'Ivoire, 70 per cent of families each own about 8 fowls on average. In Burkina Faso average ownership per person is 2.2 fowl and 1.5 guinea fowl. In Mali 79, 83 and 100 per cent of families in rainfed, irrigated and urban areas respectively own poultry, and 25–50 per cent of these own two or more species.

The housing provided to birds is usually rudimentary or non-existent, although that for pigeons is more sophisticated (Fig 13.2). Little direct feeding is practised, but there are usually fair quantities of household scraps and birds range the streets in search of other food. Mortality rates are very high.

Fig 13.2 *Housing for pigeons constructed from dried mud in a family compound in Niono town, Mali (note also the pen for rabbits in this urban system)*

Table 13.2 Clutch sizes of domestic fowl in Mali

System	Number of clutches	Clutch number						Overall
		1	2	3	4	5	6–10	
Millet	187	8.7	9.0	9.2	8.9	9.3	9.5	8.9
Rice	141	7.9	9.7	8.5	11.5	10.3	9.0	8.8
Urban	106	7.9	7.9	9.8	7.6	8.7	13.7	8.5
Total	434	8.3	9.0	9.1	9.2	9.4	9.8	8.8

Source: Wilson, R.T., Traoré, A., Traoré, A., Kuit, H.G. and Slingerland, M. 1987. Livestock production in central Mali: Reproduction, growth and mortality of domestic fowl under traditional management. *Trop. Anim. Hlth. Prod.* 19: 229–236

Fowl lay their first clutch of about 8 eggs at about 240 days. The overall clutch size under slightly different systems of management is 8.8 ± 3.1, the number of eggs increasing with age (Table 13.2). Eggs are small (34.4 ± 5.6 g), but become heavier with succeeding clutches and represent 3.4 per cent of hen weight. Intervals between clutches are about 92 days. Total annual egg production is about 36 eggs, equivalent to about 120 per cent of body weight. Hatching percentage is about 70 per cent but varies with season. Chicks hatch at about 22 g, reach 550 g at 15 weeks and are mature at over 1 year, cocks weighing 1.60 kg and hens 1.02 kg.

Guinea fowl lay more eggs (weight 41 g) than domestic fowl, which are kept mainly for meat. Many guinea fowl eggs are sold. The annual production of guinea fowl eggs is about 280 per cent of body weight. Muscovy ducks are more precocious than either fowl species, laying first at about 210 days. While clutch size is similar, eggs are much larger at about 60 g, both absolutely and as a proportion of mature body weight. Pigeons lay their first clutch of 2 eggs (each weighing 16 g) at about 4–5 months and produce about 8 clutches/year for a total output of about 80 per cent of adult weight.

Conclusions

Production is low in all species and is further reduced by high losses from neglect and disease. Reasons for the low productivity are diverse. Conventional wisdom, gleaned from the very poor data base on poultry (only 45 of 20 000 documents relating to 22 African countries in the continent's main livestock reference library are wholly or mainly about poultry) cites inadequate genetic material, poor nutrition, disease, and lack of market infrastructure. Most attempts to upgrade local types by replacing native males with superior exotic birds have failed because the latter rarely survived long enough to reproduce. Nutrition is inadequate but lack of water is probably at least as important as lack of feed. Disease is certainly a problem, not least Newcastle Disease during cold periods, but is not insurmountable. Market infrastructure is adequate but is outside the control of administrators and, therefore, thought not to be.

In Burkina Faso it has been estimated that the capital value of the poultry flock is about 7 per cent that of cattle and 33 per cent that of sheep and goats. Investments in small scale poultry improvement would undoubtedly yield good returns. The technology for intensive poultry production is easily transferred from the developed world, but this is expensive in limited foreign exchange and in other resources, and the benefits, if any, do not reach the poor. Investments in traditional poultry in Burkina Faso – virtually the only African country with a programme to improve this sector – have resulted in clutch sizes 50 per cent greater following simple veterinary inputs and 100 per cent greater with veterinary inputs and improved management. Hatching percentages have also been raised by 50 per cent, mortality reduced from 88 per cent to 72 per cent at 12 months and offtake per hen increased from 2.0 birds to 4.8–8.6.

Case study: Peri-urban milk production in Mauritania

Peri-urban and urban agriculture is not new in Africa. Vegetable plots and small intensive fattening units are found in and around all the major cities of the continent. The phenomen of rapid urbanisation, on the other hand, is new to Mauritania, where, in little more than 25 years, the percentage of nomads in the population has dropped from almost 75 per cent to about 10 per cent. A quarter of all Mauritanians now live in the capital city, Nouakchott.

Urbanisation has brought numerous social and economic changes.

- New types of livestock owners, such as retail and wholesale merchants, civil servants and military personnel, are more willing to try new methods of production.
- Milk is now produced for sale, instead of being only for home consumption. In Nouakchott it is hawked on the street, sold by door-to-door delivery, or supplied to dairy plants.
- Commercialisation is accompanied by major changes in livestock management, feeding, and veterinary care.

Around Nouakchott milk is produced mainly by camels (Fig 13.3), but there are also some cattle units and a more or less *ad hoc* system of goat milk production. In August 1993 there were an estimated 5000 female camels in about 100 herds producing milk for the city.

At the current stage of development production levels, management

Fig 13.3 *Camels in an urban dairy on the outskirts of Nouakchott, Mauritania*

and profitability are highly variable. A good manager can sell as much as 3 kg milk/lactating female/day over a lactation period of about 12 months. The best camels produce as much as 8 kg at the lactation peak. Even at this level of production, however, variable costs can approach or even exceed the value of the milk sold. But milk is not the only source of income from the operation. Camels at an advanced stage of pregnancy or having recently given birth are bought from nomadic herds at a price equivalent to an animal in poor condition that would otherwise be destined for slaughter. After a year of good management and feeding (a dry matter average of 6 kg/day high in energy and protein) the camel weighs considerably more than when she was bought and can be re-sold at a price some 50 per cent higher. In addition, there is the yearling value of her young.

The cattle enterprise is slightly different. The cows belong to the family, which often maintains a cropping operation in the south of the country. As they approach the end of their gestation they are transferred by lorry to Nouakchott, where they are kept permanently tethered in people's backyards. Water and concentrates are bought and part of the labour is hired. The roughage part of the ration is provided by rice straw and other crop by-products from the family farm, as much as 200 km away. These are again transported by lorry, which returns loaded with dry cows and the manure for spreading on the fields.

Conclusions

The system is far from perfect. There are problems with the supply of feed of adequate quality (some camels appear to be fed largely on cardboard). There is a need to ensure that the system does not create health and hygiene problems for its managers. Competition from cheap imported milk, milk powder and milk products reduces profitability. Nevertheless, the system obviously works, since there are more and more people practising it. It could be encouraged by the enactment of appropriate legislation for its protection and development and by the provision of extension advice. Its integration with an urban vegetable or forage production system would also improve both profitability and sustainability.

PART 3

**Intensive systems with high input
and high output**

14 Crop-livestock-aquaculture sustainable systems

Aquaculture

Aquaculture is the production, processing and eating or marketing of water organisms such as fish, molluscs, crustaceans and algae. About 10 million t of aquaculture output were produced annually in the late 1980s, equivalent to about 15 per cent of all commercially caught fish. It is estimated that aquaculture yield could be increased to 35 million t by the year 2000 and future possibilities appear almost unlimited.

The cultivation, as opposed to wild harvesting, of freshwater edible organisms is essentially an Asian activity. Around 85 per cent of world output comes from this region. Opportunities for production in Africa and Latin America are similar to those in Asia in terms of climate and water availability, but have so far remained neglected.

Fish ponds have been exploited in China for over 2000 years and it is probable that there has always been some integration with agriculture and livestock. Only relatively recently, however, have concerted efforts been made to develop closely integrated systems capable of producing high and sustainable yields of energy and protein for human consumption.

Levels of development and intensity
Simple

New ponds can be developed in less densely populated areas. Seasonal use of rice basins with different water for the crop and for fish is one common system in which fish yields of 300–500 kg/ha are achieved with no inputs. Stocking with non-selective feeders, such as several species of carp and cichlids, can easily increase yields to 2000 kg/flooding period.

Flooding for fish in the wet season and then using the same water for rice in the dry period is a higher level of intensity. Fish yields can be further increased if the water is deep enough for fish of different habits (littoral, pelagic and benthic feeders) and at different trophic levels (detritus feeders, macrophages, insectivores and piscivores) to be stocked. In a multi-species system of this nature fish yields as high as 12 000 kg/ ha/ year are achieved. In addition, deeper ponds reduce the quantity of water required per tonne of fish harvested to about 60 per cent of that in shallow ponds.

Highest

The most intense levels involve crops, livestock and fish (Fig 14.1). Crops in this context include aquatic plants, used not only by fish but also by people, such as *kankong* or water morning glory (*Ipomoea aquatica*) and water fern (*Azolla filiculoides*). Systems of this nature are complex and require high management standards to ensure that water depths and temperatures are maintained and that there is sufficient oxygen for the aquatic organisms to breathe. The crops (cereals and water plants), fish and shrimps, and poultry and small ruminants require constant attendance and minute adjustments to management. In return they provide a major staple grain, a green 'vegetable' harvested on a 10-day cycle, 5 or 6 harvests of fish per year (each of as much as 1000 kg/ha) and a constant supply of eggs and meat, for consumption or sale. Such a system suffers little from the marked seasonal variations in food and income prevalent in less balanced systems.

Case study: Integrated goat and fish farming in the Philippines

In the north-west of the island of Luzon about 76 per cent of the 4 million or so people of the four coastal provinces of Ilocos Norte, Ilocos Sur, La Union and Pangasinan live in rural areas. Average farm size is 1.25 ha and 21 per cent of the population are engaged in some kind of aquaculture.

Major constraints to fish pond culture have been the high cost of fertiliser and commercial feed for the fish. Dietary protein for humans, therefore, remains inadequate. The integration of goats was proposed as a means of raising productivity and incomes, creating labour opportunities, balancing protein and energy in the human diet, or improving the stability of the system.

An experiment using two levels of stocking with fish and three levels of goat stocking was set up and run for two 120-day fish cycles, covering one

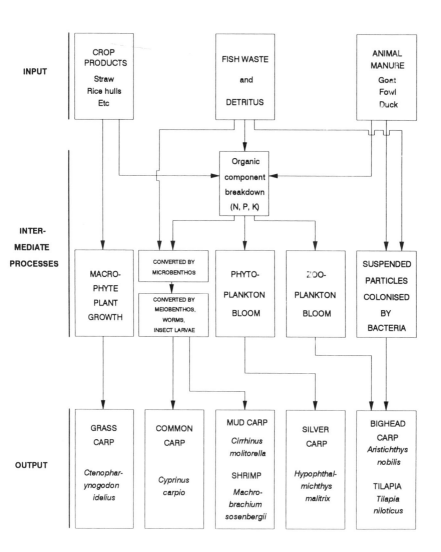

Fig 14.1 *Schematic diagram of a sustainable crop-livestock-aquaculture system (Source: adapted from Alsagoff, S.A., Clonts, H.A. and Jolly, C.M. 1990. An integral poultry, multi-species aquaculture for Malaysian rice farms: A mixed integer programming approach. Agric. Syst. 32: pp. 207–231)*

240-day goat cycle. Goat manure was the only source of fertiliser. Goat kids weighing 8.5 kg at the beginning of the trial were housed on slatted floors over the ponds. They were fed a mixture of grass and legumes in the pens.

In the first cycle, highest weights per individual fish were achieved with a combination of 300 goats/10 000 fish (Table 14.1). Maximum

Table 14.1 Goat and fish stocking rates and individual fish weights and net yields in two production cycles in an integrated aquaculture system in the Philippines

Species and stocking rate per hectare		First 120-day cycle		Second 120-day cycle	
Goat	Fish	Fish individual weight (g)	Net yield (kg/ha)	Fish individual weight (g)	Net yield (kg/ha)
0	10 000	63.7	637	66.0	660
	20 000	49.2	965	50.4	1 009
200	10 000	81.3	813	84.0	840
	20 000	53.4	1 069	62.2	1 244
300	10 000	84.8	848	87.5	875
	20 000	58.2	1 170	65.2	1 305

Source: adapted from Libunao L.P. 1990. Goat/fish integrated farming in the Philippines. *Ambio* 19: pp. 408–410

total net yields of fish were, however, higher for the 300/20 000 combination. Lowest individual weights and total net yields were obtained with no goats. Goats increased in weight from about 8.5 kg to about 16.5 kg over the 120-day period.

Similar results were obtained in the second 120-day cycle. As the goats were bigger and produced more manure, fish weights and yields were greater than in the first period.

Conclusions

In both periods, fish growth increased with the amount of manure applied, indicating that the feed produced by the manure was being efficiently utilised. Economic analysis showed higher net returns with the 300/20 000 combination, providing profits about three times greater than the 0/10 000 combination. Larger fish tend to fetch higher prices per unit weight than do smaller ones, so the 300/10 000 combination (or perhaps an even higher density of goats to the lower fish density) may become more profitable.

Case study: Sustainable intensive production in Colombia

Sugar cane, multi-purpose nitrogen-fixing permanent tree crops and water plants produce high levels of biomass. Pigs and ducks can convert unconventional high-moisture feed resources such as cane juice and water plants into meat and eggs. Unlike ruminants, they produce little methane in relation to their meat output and thus contribute little to global warming.

Farming systems developed along these lines in Colombia (Fig 14.2) have shown themselves able to produce very high levels of livestock output; as much as 3000 kg meat/ha/year. Cane stalk, after removing the tops, is converted to juice and bagasse using animal draught power. The juice can be incorporated in pig and duck diets at up to 75 per cent of the ration, completely replacing cereal grains. The tops are fed to sheep. The tree foliage is separated into leaves and twigs and the leaves, together with azolla from the pond, provide protein feed to both the ruminants and the monogastrics. The bagasse and the twigs are used as fuel. The animal excreta are recycled through biogas digesters, ponds and earthworms to provide additional household fuel, protein feed for livestock, and organic fertiliser and humus for the crops.

The high-biomass sugar cane varieties used are harvested on a 12-month cycle, the dead leaves being left as mulch for the soil. The decaying process, aided by bacteria and fungi, fixes up to 100 kg N/ha/

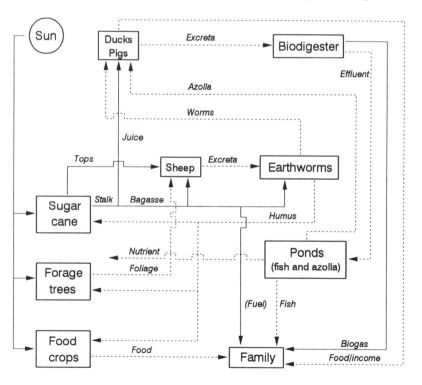

Fig 14.2 *Schematic diagram of an integrated sustainable mixed farming system (Source: adapted from Preston T.R. 1993. Sustainable intensive livestock systems for the humid tropics.* World Anim. Rev. *72: pp. 2–8)*

year. A variety of multi-purpose trees, chosen to provide feed throughout the year and to occupy the various soil types, produce protein for livestock. In Colombia the species used are *Gliricidia sepium*, *Trichanthera gigantea* and *Erythrina fusca*. *Leucaena leucocephala* is not used because of the high cost of harvesting in this cut-and-carry system. Some 2 ha of cane produce 240 t of stalk, which yields 120 t of juice and 120 t of bagasse, equivalent to 816 MJ of fuel energy. The 0.14 ha of multi-purpose trees produces 8.2 t of edible foliage for livestock.

A pig fattened from 25 kg to 90 kg eats 1200 kg of cane juice, 53 kg of soya grain and 560 kg of *Azolla filiculoides*. In addition to meat it produces 0.5 kg of methane. A duck fattened from 700 g to 2.5 kg eats about 18 kg of juice and 3.2 kg of supplement. The 60 t of tops produced by the cane, together with tree foliage, provide the basic diet for a flock of 30 hair sheep and their young. The sheep also use molasses-urea blocks, poultry manure and rice polishings (Table 14.2). Ewes produce 1.9 lambs/year from a litter of 2.22 young 1.53 times per year, and the total lamb live weight produced for sale is 972 kg. The sheep also produce 100 kg of methane.

The ponds are used to grow azolla fern as well as produce fish. The fern can provide as much as 50 per cent of the protein needs of the pigs, 30 of which need 240 kg/day which can be provided by 1500 m^2 of pond surface. Fresh earthworms, of which 6 kg/year can be produced from 1 m^3 of manure, complement the azolla and a mixture of 50:50 of the two can replace half the soya in a juice-based diet for poultry.

Table 14.2   Estimated inputs and outputs of an integrated mixed farming system in Colombia

Sub-system	Inputs	Outputs
Biomass	2 ha sugar cane 0.14 ha *Gliricidia sepium*	60 t (816MJ) bagasse
Pig fattening	80 weaner pigs @ 25 kg (2000 kg) 4240 kg supplement	7200 kg pig live weight 40 kg methane
Duck fattening	1200 ducklings @ 0.7 kg (840 kg) 3840 kg supplement	3000 kg duck live weight 12 kg methane
Sheep rearing and fattening	30 sheep 1280 kg molasses-urea block 2160 kg poultry litter 222 kg rice polishings	972 kg lamb live weight 100 kg methane
Net live weight		4160 kg

Source: Preston T.R. 1993. Sustainable intensive livestock systems for the humid tropics. *World Anim. Rev.* 72: pp. 2–8

Conclusions

The system is friendly to the environment. Biodigester effluent, sheep manure and earthworm humus supply the required plant nutrients. Dead leaves from the cane and trees are used as a mulch to improve fertility and prevent soil erosion. The system is designed for resource-poor farmers, to whom it provides ample employment. Indeed, it is specially suited to their needs, since all the resources used can be produced on the farm itself, incurring minimal dependence on external inputs.

15 Intensive production of monogastric species

Poultry meat and eggs, and also pig meat where there are no taboos against its being used, can be a valuable source of protein in human diets. In theory the rapid technological advances achieved for the intensive production of both these species in recent years are readily transferable. However, these technologies are costly in management skills, in high-quality feed resources, in housing and equipment and very often in limited foreign exchange. They remain attractive to development planners in many countries because of their impressive production figures. Such figures are often presented very persuasively by representatives of the multi-national agri-businesses that have developed this type of production to an exact science. In these systems 'standards' are usually set, for example for egg production and eggs per hen housed (Fig 15.1) or for grams of gain per day and per unit feed.

The attractions of such systems in countries with a protein deficit are obvious. The disadvantages, in massive capital outlay and low production (or complete failure due to machinery breakdown, interruptions in feed supply or wrong medication, which have occurred in some cases) become apparent only later. Successes have been achieved in some countries, notably with poultry in the Arab states, and these have persuaded governments to invest, or to encourage private companies to invest, usually with promises of support and tax-free benefits.

In the early stages of intensive poultry development it is usual for day-old chicks to be imported for either egg or meat production. The chicks are housed in the already prepared facilities. At a more advanced stage hatcheries may be set up to incubate eggs supplied by the agri-businesses. Finally, it is the ambition of developing countries to have their own parent and grand-parent stock so that all operations from breeding to finished product can be controlled.

Case study: Intensive poultry development in Pakistan

At independence in 1947 there was one government poultry farm in each of Pakistan's four provinces. These farms were supposed to produce Rhode Island Red and White Leghorn birds for distribution to small-scale producers, to replace the indigenous Desi chicken. In 1963 the national airline collaborated with a Canadian agri-business to set up egg and meat production to supply the expanding Karachi market. Other agri-businesses soon followed and by 1968 commercial poultry numbered 0.6 million layers and 1.7 million broilers. A miniature boom followed – ten hatcheries and three feed mills were established.

During the 1970s government provided further incentives to the intensive poultry industry and since then there have been massive increases in investment and production (Table 15.1). A directorate of poultry production and several poultry research institutes have been created. Government assistance to the private sector includes free advice on management, feeding and disease control including free vaccines and other medicines. Institutional and financial assistance is provided through 'soft' leases of land for poultry enterprises, tax breaks, concessional rates for electricity, duty-free imports and the stabilisation of maize and sorghum feed prices.

Highly productive layers bred mainly from White Leghorns produce

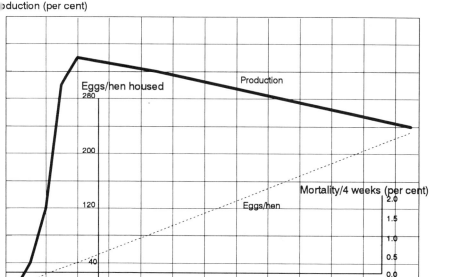

Fig 15.1 *An example of an agri-business production schedule for intensive layer poultry production*

Table 15.1 Intensification of poultry production in Pakistan, 1977–1986

Parameter		Year		Increase (%)
		1977	1986	
Investment (million rupees)		915	5 000	446
Hatcheries:	number	23	110	378
	production capacity (millions)	38	110	378
	actual production (millions)	28	78	176
Breeding farms:	number	30	241	703
	production capacity (millions)	0.31	1.52	390
	actual production (millions)	0.22	0.91	315
Layer farms:	number	1 450	4 060	180
	bird capacity (millions)	4.25	12.00	182
	bird numbers (millions)	3.32	9.50	186
	eggs produced (millions)	730	2 280	212
Broiler farms:	number	725	4 236	484
	bird capacity (millions)	11.5	60.1	423
	bird numbers (millions)	8.8	55.0	587
	meat produced (t)[1]	7 610	52 250	587
Village production:	bird numbers (millions)	33.5	49.8	49
	eggs produced (millions)	1 036	1 690	63
	meat produced (millions)	38 110	61 060	60

Note:
1   Does not include 2660 t of meat in 1977 and 7290 t in 1986 from culled layers and breeding birds

Source: adapted from Kazni, S.E. 1987. An overview of poultry breeding in Pakistan. In: *Poultry breeding, breed performance and breed management in the Near East*. Food and Agriculture Organisation: Amman, Jordan: pp. 24–34   .

an average of 200–240 eggs/year. Broilers capable of reaching 1.25 kg at 8 weeks are also raised but are generally marketed at about 1.00 kg because of local preferences.

Conclusions

Investment costs have increased more than output, but much of the investment has been for hatchery and breeding farms and may be recovered in the future.

The success of intensive production has had some spin-off for the traditional sector, where improved tropical breeds have been introduced for cross-breeding and where the fowl population increased from 33 million to 50 million between 1977 and 1986. The availability of poultry products increased over the same period from 23 to 40 eggs/person/year and from 0.64 to 1.21 kg of meat.

Case study: State pig production in Cuba

The pig industry in Cuba is highly centralised. In 1988, on a little over 100 state-owned and -managed farms there were 92 000 sows, or more than 800 sows/ farm. By 1995 it is expected that at least 50 new farms will house 2000 sows each. Farms operate a continuous weekly schedule of insemination, births and production of feeder pigs. Pigs are weaned on a Thursday, at about 33 days old, and fed, in two-tiered metal cages, to 100 days on a complete, cereal-based dry ration. Feeder pigs, with a total weight of 55 t/week, are shipped to feedlots at 100 days old and/or at 25–28 kg. On transfer to the feedlot they are fed a diet based on swill for a further 147 days.

The Large White (or Yorkshire) is the basic maternal breed and Landrace, Duroc, Hampshire and Lacombe are the sire lines. Only 5 per cent of sows are purebred, these being at the summit of a pyramid breeding system of genetic selection and improvement. Lower down the pyramid are 14 per cent of females which are used to produce crossbred replacement gilts (mainly Landrace or Duroc males on Large White females) and lower still 81 per cent of crossbred sows which are put to purebred males to produce the feeder pigs.

The 200-sow units already in existence house 25 000 pigs at any one time. Average litter size in 1988 was 9.3 live pigs, with 77 per cent fertility and each sow producing young live weight of 1.3 t/year. Artificial insemination represented 20 per cent of all matings. Average slaughter weight at 247 days was 87 kg.

Immediately after service, gestating sows are fed 1 kg of a dry mixture containing 22 per cent protein, and a further 2 kg of B molasses. Just before farrowing they are switched to 4.5 kg of a dry ration with 18 per cent protein, this continuing until piglets are weaned at 33 days. Feed is reduced to 2.5 kg until the return to oestrus and service again. Molasses is not fed except during pregnancy and each sow consumes 500 kg/ year of this as well as 700 kg of the protein feed.

A swill-based diet is fed to 75 per cent of the feeder pigs in the fattening units, a diet of 1.6 kg protein supplement and 1.4 kg B molasses is used for a further 15 per cent and the remaining animals receive a diet based on protein molasses. In the first system, swill and B molasses are mixed in a ratio of about 8:1. This mixture contains 22–23 per cent solids with 14–15 per cent protein in the dry matter. Pigs eat about 8 kg/day of this mixture and about 0.8 kg of dry feed. Total consumption per pig to slaughter is 1200 kg of swill and 120 kg/day of dry feed. It is estimated that this represents a saving of about 500 kg of dry feed, almost all of which has to be imported.

Conclusions

It is hoped to double pig production in Cuba over a 7-year period. Swill will continue to be important but, as it is unlikely that the quantity will increase in line with projected pig numbers, increased use will be made of molasses (fortified by yeast-produced proteins) and other sugar products including fermented cane juice. It is expected that future developments will help to improve the daily weight gains, currently slow by world standards. Some four years into the pig development plan, however, it appeared that progress was not in line with the master plan. In May 1991 the Cuban authorities imposed a weekly ration of 100 g of meat on every person in the country.

16 Microlivestock systems

The term microlivestock is used to describe a wide range of small breeds of domestic animals. The species considered in this book are:

* rabbits;
* guinea pigs;
* cane rats; and
* snails.

Other species include, among some 150 candidates, rodents, reptiles, insects and earthworms.

Microlivestock play important roles where land is scarce and large groups of people, particularly women and children, are deprived of adequate income and nutrition. They occupy economic niches not readily available to larger species. They are particularly useful for people on the margins of the cash economy because they cost less to buy, represent less of a financial risk, produce a faster return on investment, allow flexibility of operations, provide a steady source of food or income, are easily transportable, and are often very efficient converters of feed. Other benefits include efficient use of space, low capital requirements for housing facilities, use of unconventional feed resources, easy management, and numerous by-products such as fur and skins.

Microlivestock have been neglected by research and development in the past for several reasons, notably the large number of species involved and the specialised nature of the niches they occupy, which makes it difficult to decide how best to invest limited resources. However, their potential is now being more generally recognised and their future should be assured.

Case study: Snails

In the tropics snails are of most importance as human food in Africa, where they are eaten over much of the humid west coast area and in central-west Africa as far south as northern Angola. In Europe the edible snail is of the genus *Helix* but in Africa the main edible species are of the family Achatinidae.

Commonly known in English as giant African snails, those farmed or gathered for human food comprise two genera, each of three species. *Achatina* is the most sought after genus, the largest species being *A. achatina* which is distributed along the West African coast from Guinea to Cameroon in the humid forest areas. *A. balleata*, is somewhat smaller and has a less conspicuously marked shell; there appears to be an isolated population of this species in Sierra Leone, but it is mainly found in Cameroon, Equatorial Guinea, Gabon, Congo, Zaire and Angola. *A. monochromatien* is similar to *A. balteata* and is found only in southern Benin. A species originally indigenous to the coasts of Tanzania and Kenya, *A. fulica*, is not eaten there but has spread with commerce to south-east Asia and the Pacific islands. This last species has become a pest in some parts of the Far East.

Three species of the genus *Archachatina* are also found in West Africa. These snails are smaller than *Achatina* and are not as popular for human food. The most widespread is *A. marginata*, which is distributed from Nigeria to Zaire. The two other species have more restricted distribution, *A. ventricosa* occurring from Sierra Leone to Côte d'Ivoire and *A. degneri* from Ghana to Benin.

Snails are hermaphrodites, but cross-fertilisation between two individuals is the rule. *A. achatina* becomes sexually mature and lays its first eggs at 7–11 months. The other two *Achatina* species mature later. Eggs are first laid 8–20 days after mating, but several clutches are laid from a single mating over a period of months. Size and number of eggs vary among clutches, but the *Achatina* spp. generally lay 140–180 small eggs/clutch while *Archachatina* lay 6–12 larger ones. The period from egg laying to hatching is about 6–7 weeks, although the hatching period within a clutch may be prolonged. Hatching in the wild is successful in about 50 per cent of cases, but this can be improved under controlled conditions (for example 77 per cent when the eggs are kept on a damp cloth).

The hatching weight of *Archachatina marginata* is about 2.1 g, with a weekly gain of about 0.85 g to reach about 35 g at 40 weeks. *Achatina achatina* has a mature body weight in the range 200–350 g at 3 years.

Snails are omnivorous feeders and will eat wild and cultivated plants; hence their potential as pests. Many small species of snail feed on decomposing material and detritus as well as greenstuff. In spite of their eclectic dietary tastes, snails may not be very efficient users of organic waste under controlled conditions as they can be very selective feeders.

The natural habitat of snails is damp ground with undergrowth. During dry spells free-living snails are able to aestivate by reducing mobility,

Fig 16.1 *Snails (lower left) on sale at a local market in Lomé, Togo (note also the grilled grasscutters in a basin in the centre of the photograph)*

reproductive behaviour and growth. Water is conserved by sealing the shell opening with an epiphragma. Under controlled conditions humidity needs to be high to ensure optimum performance.

In West Africa most snails that reach the market are caught wild (Fig 16.1). There are several links in the marketing chain. Snails provide a source of subsistence food as well as income. Urban consumers are prepared to pay twice as much for snails as for red meat. The price in Abidjan, Côte d'Ivoire, where the annual consumption is estimated at 1000 t/year, was about $US2/kg in 1986. In view of the size of the market there must be some concern for the long-term survival of the snails.

Approximately 38 per cent of total weight is consumable, this representing the foot (the shell is equivalent to 26 per cent, viscera 16 per cent and blood and slime 18 per cent of total weight). Moisture content of the edible portion is 73 per cent, with 18 per cent being protein. The nitrogen-free extract is 5 per cent while fat, fibre and ash together comprise less than 3 per cent of the foot weight. Calcium, magnesium, potassium and iron are important mineral elements in the foot. The protein content of the edible portion of the snail is higher than that of ruminants and is similar to that of the giant cane rat and poultry. The fat content is low but NFE (nitrogen-free extract) is high. The energy content is about 334 kJ/100 g, which may be compared with the 836 kJ/100 g in poultry.

Conclusions

Snail farming on an extensive open or more intensive closed or semi-closed system has proved feasible both in Europe and in Africa. The extensive system represents a natural development from gathering. Snails are kept in enclosures until after breeding and then fattened on a variety of sown crops, including turnips (*Brassica napus*), burdock (*Arctium lappa*), herbaceous plantain (*Plantago lanceolata*) and lettuce, chicory and Jerusalem artichoke. Fattened snails are sold during the dry season when prices are high and young are either returned to the wild to grow out or kept in an enclosed intensive system. Intensive systems are more difficult to manage and need to take account of location and market factors as well as possible repercussions arising from their offensive smell.

Case study: Cane rats and grasscutters

Cane rats or African giant rats of the genus *Cricetomys* and grasscutters of the genus *Thryonomys* are widespread throughout Africa in all except the driest areas. They appear to be commoner in West Africa than elsewhere, but possibly this is an illusion due to their use there as food.

The cane rat used as food in West Africa is *Cricetomys gambianus*. It is a burrow-dwelling species, usually solitary, and apparently prefers damp places, although the few published reports on its ecology are conflicting. The species of grasscutter found in West Africa is *Thryonomys swinderianus*. It is a non-burrowing rodent of large size.

Puberty in the cane rat occurs at about 23–24 weeks, the oestrus cycle is 4 days and the gestation period about 28 days. Litter size is about 3 young, and 6 litters a year are possible. The grasscutter breeds all the year round in Ghana but appears to have only 1 litter/year. The gestation period is very long, about 155 days, this probably being related to development of the young at birth.

Cane rats are medium-sized rodents weighing approximately 1 kg at maturity. Daily weight gains under experimental conditions average about 10 g from 4 to 10 weeks old. The young are virtually helpless at birth; they have no fur and the eyes do not open until about 21 days. In contrast, the young of the grasscutter are born at an advanced stage; the eyes are already open and they are fully furred and capable of moving and feeding themselves shortly after birth. Mature weights of grasscutters are as much as 6.8 kg.

Like many other rodents, both the cane rat and the grasscutter are mainly herbivorous but will take many different kinds of food. In the wild the cane rat appears to eat mainly palm fruits and tubers, particularly yams, along with a variety of other fruits, seeds and insects. There seem

118

to be some differences in dietary preferences between males and females. In captivity the cane rat will eat yam peels, cassava peels, plantain peels, maize chaff and cocoyam and yam tubers with apparent digestibilities of 12–72 per cent of the dry matter at a feed conversion ratio of 2.6–3.3.

Male cane rats with an average live weight of 1033 g and females averaging 919 g killed out at 51.5 per cent with low fat and relatively high protein contents. Grasscutters kill out at as much as 64 per cent with a meat to bone ratio of 3.5:1.0, the flesh comprising 70 per cent moisture, 19 per cent protein, 9 per cent ether extract and 1 per cent ash.

Conclusions

Most cane rats and grasscutters used for domestic consumption or sold commercially are captured from the wild. In most West African countries these rodents command a higher price (weight for weight) than do domestic red meat animals and poultry. Wild stock are being depleted owing to direct predation for food and to generate income, as well as indirect predation as the area under cultivation to crops expands.

Several trials have shown the feasibility of domesticating both species. In captivity, the rodents show psychological problems such as extreme aggression towards each other and fear of their keepers, down to the fourth generation. At these early stages, cannibalism of the young by the parents, especially the male, is common and as many as 40 per cent of animals may be lost. In Nigeria, animals kept in suitable housing and adequately fed have been bred down to the fifteenth generation. In Benin a successful development project has communal pens for breeding and growing stock but finishes animals for sale in individual cages.

Case study: Rabbits

Rabbits belong to several genera in the sub-families Leporinae (which includes the similar hares, *Lepus* spp.) and Palaeologinae. The Rodentia are the second order in the Glives. Species of rabbit are distributed over most of the world's major land masses. Most, if not all, rabbits in the broad sense have developed a system of digestion which serves a similar function to rumination. They partially digest their feed; the voided faeces are then reingested and final digestion takes place, this process technically being known as coprophagy.

The true rabbit, *Oryctolagus cuniculus*, has several sub-species and was originally native to south-west Europe and North Africa. It was known to the Phoenicians in Spain about 3000 BC and the Romans spread it throughout their empire as a game animal. At a later stage it was kept in stone-walled parks or pens, sometimes called *leporaria*, to provide sport, and the fetuses and newborn rabbits, known as laurices, were consumed by the Romans and later by monks. These *leporaria* are the origins of some of the warrens where large numbers of rabbits are still found. Rabbits have been introduced to other areas in modern times by people, notably Australia where (as elsewhere) they are regarded as a serious pest, competing with common domestic herbivores for grazing.

The rabbit was truly domesticated about 400 years ago but it was not until the feudal system was abolished in Europe that the keeping of rabbits in hutches or cages became widespread. As domestic animals rabbits have undergone several cycles of popularity and decline. They have been popular in times of war in Europe when other types of meat were not easily available. The rabbit's precocity and prolificacy enable very rapid population expansion. Europe remains the centre of rabbit production, with the former USSR producing more than 200 000 t of carcass meat in 1980, and France, Italy and Spain more than 100 000 t each. Annual consumption/person, however, is highest in tropical and sub-tropical countries: Malta (4.30 kg), Cyprus (0.89 kg), Egypt (0.22 kg), Ghana (0.20 kg), Perú (0.13 kg), Algeria and Colombia (0.12 kg each) and Mexico (0.06 kg).

Rabbit husbandry is being encouraged in many poorer tropical countries:

• they are relatively easy to rear;
• rabbits can be managed in small units; and
• they do not necessarily compete directly for human food.

Wild rabbits are gregarious, sedentary animals which maintain a territory that varies in size according to the feed supply. The territory is marked with urine. Rabbits dig underground burrows, or warrens, to which they retreat at the slightest alarm. At parturition females withdraw to a private burrow where the young are born and are normally suckled once a day. Females outnumber males in wild societies and, whether they have young of their own or not, attack the young of other individuals. These general considerations are important for housing design and construction in captivity. In the wild, danger is signalled by the first rabbit to notice it, by thumping the hind foot, a sign at which all the members of the society rapidly take evasive action by disappearing into the warren. Disturbances in rabbitries can elicit similar reactions and can greatly affect productivity.

Female rabbits usually attain puberty at 70–75 per cent of adult weight and can breed at 4 months of age. Under natural conditions in the temperate zones there is considerable seasonality in reproduction, probably resulting from the combined effects of day length and temperature. In the tropics, temperature would appear to be the most important variable.

Female rabbits are induced ovulators, eggs being shed following stimulation by coitus. Does are considered to be in oestrus when they accept service and in dioestrus when they do not. Does in oestrus adopt a characteristic back-down, hindquarter-raised posture. Unlike most species, pregnant rabbits will accept mating, and by the 20th day of the 31–32 day gestation period, 80 per cent of does return to heat. Simultaneous pregnancies at different stages of development (superfoetation) occur in the hare but are not known in the rabbit. Spermatogenesis in male rabbits begins at 6–7 weeks but spermatozoa do not occur in the ejaculate until about 15 weeks.

Rabbit litters may be as large as 20 young, but 3–12 is a common range. Mortality rates are very high under natural conditions. Growth is rapid in surviving young. Milk production is at a maximum at about 3 weeks after parturition and ceases by about 7 weeks. Rabbit milk is very rich, with 26 per cent dry matter, nearly 10 per cent fat and 14 per cent proteins. Rabbits are principally grazers in the wild but will accept a variety of feeds under domestication, where very high rates of weight gain can be achieved.

Rabbits produce meat, skins and Angora wool. Most tropical production is for meat, mainly for home consumption. China exports about 30 000 t/year of meat to the European Union. Uruguay has a small export trade, about 40 t in 1980. Australia exports some rabbit skins from wild animals killed in control operations and it is possible that a small proportion of these originate in the tropics. Angora wool occupies a special position in the world textile trade. China is by far the largest producer of Angora wool at about 2000 t/year. Argentina, Korea and India also produce small amounts. There is a very small Angora rabbit wool industry in Bolivia (Fig 16.2) where yields of 100–150 g fibre are produced every 70 days, the product being sold for export at about $US30/kg in early 1991.

Fig 16.2 *Angora rabbits being tested for fibre production at Oruro in western Bolivia*

Modern fast growing breeds of rabbit are capable of reaching live weights of 2.2 kg at 80–90 days. Dressing percentages are in the region of 60–70 per cent and increase with age, apparently independently of weight. The higher value hindquarters and loins comprise about three-fifths of the carcass. The carcass yield is slightly less in animals fed bulk roughage feeds, as this tends to cause development of the digestive tract.

Rabbit meat usually has a bland flavour. As in meat of other species, tenderness reduces as animals age and juiciness depends largely on the fat content. Protein in rabbit meat is higher than in most other meats at about 21 per cent. Rabbit meat is low in fat (8 per cent), has a low proportion of stearic and oleic acids and a high proportion of polyunsaturated linolenic and linoleic acids. Some vitamins, notably nicotinic acid and calcium pantothurate, are higher in rabbits than in other meats and minerals calcium and phosphorus are also high. Rabbit meat is, therefore, a good source of protein and some other essential nutritional elements and is relatively low, at 670 kJ/100 g meat, in energy.

Rabbits have proved easily adaptable to the intensive management systems used for caged fowl. Hybrid lines have developed very rapidly in Europe, particularly in France, and are capable of high reproductive rates and very good feed to meat conversion ratios (Table 16.1). Control of the reproductive rate and maximisation of its potential are the major factors affecting productivity.

It is possible to manage rabbits at three basic levels of reproductive

Table 16.1 Production characteristics and trends in intensive rabbit systems in Europe

Parameter	Year			
	1950	**1960**	**1970**	**1980**
Number sold/breeding female/year	<25	30	45	60
Interval between litters (days)	>90	70	54	42
Ratio concentrate feed: gain		6.0	4.5	3.6
Rabbit type	Unselected	Pure breeds	Pure breeds × improved bucks	Hybrids
Labour hours/doe/year	16.0	16.0	10.0	7.5
Labour (min)/carcass (kg)	27.0	22.0	9.5	6.2
Unit size	80–100	100–150	200–250	350–1000

Source: adapted from Lebas, F., Coudert, P., Rouvier, R. and de Rochambeau, H. 1986. *The rabbit. Husbandry, health and production.* Food and Agriculture Organisation: Rome, Italy

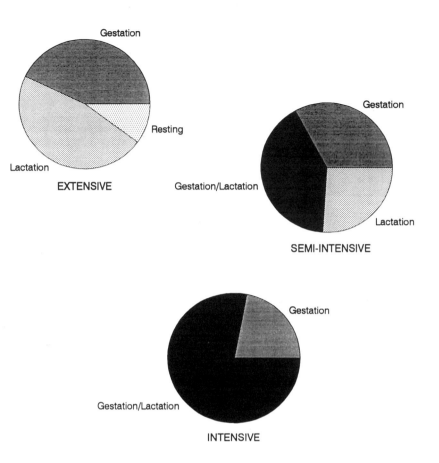

Fig 16.3 *Levels of reproductive intensity in modern rabbit husbandry systems (Source: adapted from Lebas, F., Coudert, P., Rouvier, R. and de Rochambeau, H. 1986.* The rabbit. Husbandry, health and production. *Food and Agriculture Organisation: Rome, Italy)*

rhythm (Fig 16.3). In the extensive system gestation and lactation are separate, sequential events. Young are weaned naturally at 5–6 weeks, does are bred following weaning and they give birth once in 2.5 months. In semi-intensive reproductive cycles, does are bred at 10–20 days after parturition and young are weaned at 4–5 weeks, so there is some overlapping of gestation with lactation, but about 60–65 per cent of the time the doe is either only pregnant or only lactating. In intensive systems it is usual to serve does on the day of parturition or, at the latest, 4 days afterwards. Weaning should take place not later than 28 days after parturition, and it is possible to achieve a reproductive cycle of less than 35 days.

The most intensive breeding system should be attempted only where feed conditions are optimal. Many progressive breeders modify the cycle as a function of feed and also the condition of the doe. Females giving birth to 7–8 young are usually mated immediately, while those that have large litters of 10 or more are held back for a few days.

Feed intake and nutritional requirements vary with age and particularly with reproductive status (Fig 16.4). Less energy is required in warm than in cold conditions and at 30 °C the energy demand can be 50 per cent lower than at 5 °C but weight gains are also reduced by about 30 per cent. Water requirements are greater at higher temperatures.

The rabbit is sometimes a selective feeder, but will eat a wide variety of plants. For modern systems standards have been established for animals at different stages of production (Table 16.2). Protein quality, determined by levels of essential amino acids (especially methionine, lysine and arginine), is as important as quantity, and unbalanced proteins reduce

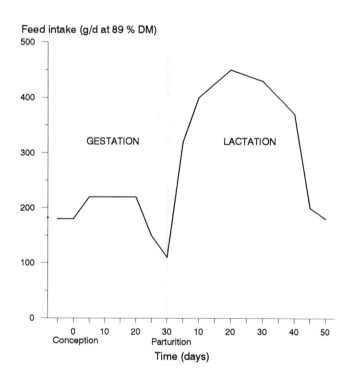

Fig 16.4   *Feed intake of rabbits at different stages of the production cycle (Source: adapted from Lebas, F., Coudert, P., Rouvier, R. and de Rochambeau, H. 1986. The* rabbit. Husbandry, health and production. *Food and Agriculture Organisation: Rome, Italy)*

Table 16.2 Nutritional requirements[1] of rabbits in different physiological states

Feed component	Physiological state			
	Growing (4–12 weeks)	Lactating	Pregnant	Dry doe
Crude protein (%)	16	18	16	13
Crude fibre (%)	14	12	14	16
Indigestible crude fibre (%)	12	10	12	13
Fat (%)	3	3	3	3
Calcium (%)	0.4	1.1	0.8	0.4
Phosphorus (%)	0.3	0.8	0.5	0.3
Iron (ppm)	50	100	50	50
Manganese (ppm)	8.5	2.5	2.5	2.5
Vitamin A (IU/kg)	6 000	12 000	12 000	6 000
Vitamin K (ppm)	0	2	2	0
Niacin (ppm)	50	0	0	0
Digestible energy (kJ/kg)	10 460	10 878	10 460	9 204
Metabolisable energy (kJ/kg)	10 040	10 460	10 400	8 870

Note:
1   Minerals and vitamins have been selected to show range in values at different stages

Source: adapted from Lebas, F., Coudert, P., Rouvier, R. and de Rochambeau, H. (1986). *The rabbit. Husbandry, health and production.* Food and Agriculture Organisation: Rome, Italy

growth rates by as much as 14 per cent and increase feed conversion ratios. Attempts to replace true proteins with non-protein nitrogen, such as urea, have not been successful with rabbits.

Rabbits grow best on compound feeds which provide 0.9–1.0 MJ DE (digestible energy)/kg $W^{0.75}$. Lactating does require as much as 1.5 MJ DE/kg $W^{0.75}$. To achieve these values the energy density needs to be in the range of 9.2–13.4 MJ DE/kg of feed. In lower intensity and smallholder systems, many local plants can be used to reduce costs. In Malawi a roughage supplement of *Amaranthus* (20 per cent protein) to a concentrate ration of 39.5 per cent maize grain, 26.0 per cent maize bran, 34.0 per cent groundnut cake and 0.5 per cent salt enabled does to produce 20 young/year and young rabbits to grow at 15 g/day for up to 16 weeks. Groundnut haulms are fed in Burkina Faso, as well as *Brachiaria ruziziensis*, and *B. mutica* is commonly used in the Philippines. In Ghana, leaves and peel of cassava have been used successfully, but both require balancing with protein and fibrous feeds. Bananas, coconuts, prickly pear, potatoes and many legumes and grasses are also fed in the tropics.

In the Caribbean rabbits are kept by small farmers and landless labourers. The small amount of capital required, the local availability of feed and the use of surplus household labour make rabbit rearing an attractive and often profitable operation. Rabbit meat is only a small proportion of total meat consumption in the West Indies, but, as elsewhere, it increases at times of economic difficulty.

Productivity is less in the Caribbean than in the most intensive production systems (Table 16.3). However, given the conditions, it is still reasonable and could be considerably improved with better management and increased inputs.

Table 16.3 Rabbit performance in the Caribbean

Trait	Unit	Mean
Reproduction		
Litter size (total young)	Number	5.0
Litter size (born alive)	Number	4.5
Litter size (weaned)	Number	3.5
Pre-weaning mortality	%	20
Age at first mating	Months	6.0
Period between parturitions	Days	80
Litters/year	Number	4
Young/doe/year	Number	12–16
Reproductive life	Months	12–18
Age at culling	Months	18–24
Growth		
Birth weight	g	45
Weaning weight (28 days)	g	320
Weight at 13 weeks	g	1600
Pre-weaning daily gain	g	10
Post-weaning daily gain	g	22
Mature weight	g	3000
Dressing % at 13 weeks		52
Post-weaning feed efficiency (concentrate: gain)		3.6

Source: Rastogi, R.K. 1990. Rabbit production in the Caribbean with special reference to Trinidad (West Indies). *Proc. 6ᵗʰ Int. Conf. Inst. Trop. Vet. Med.* pp. 252–255

Factors militating against rabbit production in the Caribbean include:

- lack of government support policies;
- inadequate marketing and processing channels;
- lack of extension services;
- inadequate adaptive research for local feed, health and management conditions;
- and a limited supply of high-performance breeding stock.

Conclusions

This small species is suitable for traditional smallholder systems of production as well as for more intensive, modern operations. Rabbits produce high-quality protein for human consumption and their value, which is complementary to other animals, is now being recognised.

Case study: Guinea pigs

Guinea pigs belong to the genus *Cavia* in the family Cavidae. There are several wild species of varying sizes in Latin America, all of which are known under the common English name of cavies. The domesticated guinea pig is also sometimes known as the cavy, probably a corruption of the Quechan *cuy*, the onomatopoeic word used by these South American Indians, because of the animal's alarm call.

The domestic species, *Cavia procellus*, is native to the Andean region of South America. It had already been domesticated by the aboriginal population of the highlands of Peru, Ecuador and Colombia by the time the Spaniards arrived. The guinea pig is a small animal, rarely weighing more than 1 kg at maturity, with short ears and no external tail although there are five caudal vertebrae. It is very variable in colour. It does not burrow although it has four strong claws on its front feet and three on its hind feet.

Several types have been developed under domestication:

- Peruvian – a variety with long silky hair and somewhat larger than other varieties;
- English or Bolivian breed – a short-haired type; and
- Abyssinian – a type having hair in a series of whorls.

Guinea pigs are gregarious and generally live in small family groups, making their dwellings of straw or other vegetative material above ground. They are intrinsically shy, but under domestication have become habituated to humans and, indeed, live apparently happily as commensals in their owners' houses.

Guinea pigs are precocious. Females are capable of breeding at 2–3 months and normally do so in traditional management systems in South America. The life span rarely exceeds 2 years but, even with a rather long gestation period of 63–75 days, a total of 7 or 8 litters/lifetime is not unusual. The litter size is in the range 1–5, but is usually 2 for primiparous females and 3 or 4 for multiparous ones. Young are born at an advanced stage of development, with full fur and their eyes open, and capable of feeding on green feed almost immediately. Weaning takes place naturally at about 14 days, by which time the dams are again pregnant.

Growth is rapid in relation to life span and mature weights are reached

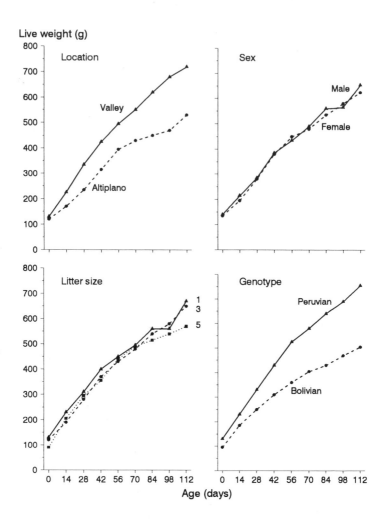

Fig 16.5 *Patterns of growth as affected by various factors in guinea pigs in Bolivia (Source: personal communication 1991)*

at about 3.5 months. The growth rate is affected by a number of factors, including litter size, breed and location but not by gender (Fig 16.5).

Guinea pigs dress out at about 65 per cent. The meat, unlike that of rabbits, is very dark in colour and has a strong but pleasant gamey taste. The hair is removed with boiling water but the animal is then cooked in its skin. The meat is low in fat and reported to have low cholesterol levels, which is one of the reasons for its increasing popularity in urban markets.

Fig 16.6   *Guinea pigs in a modern management system at the Technical University of Oruro, Bolivia*

Conclusions

In the western world the guinea pig is kept as a pet and is an important laboratory animal. In its native South America the animal is a major source of food for the indigenous population. Almost all guinea pigs are kept by South American *campesinos* for their own consumption. A small specialist market has developed in some of the larger Andean cities. There are estimated to be 20 million guinea pigs in Peru, producing about 16 000 t/year of meat, which is equivalent to about 80 per cent of sheep meat output. The animal requires, and is given, little in the way of special housing or care. Much of the wheat grown on the Andean Altiplano is cultivated especially for guinea pigs. It is cut green and fed to them in this state, a method of feeding which relieves the owners of the need to provide water.

Attempts are being made to develop more intensive systems of production (Fig 16.6). Results so far have shown breed differences in productivity and also that despite being a high-altitude species, the guinea pig reproduces and grows better at lower than at high altitudes.

PART 5

Integrating livestock and crop systems

17 Enhancing crop-livestock interactions

Until about the mid-1970s, the advantages of integrating crop and livestock production in tropical smallholder farming systems had largely escaped the attention of research and development. Since that time there has been a gradual change in emphasis, with more attention paid to the livestock component and its links with the cropping enterprise. This has coincided with the emergence of sustainability and equity issues as legitimate concerns of the research process, and with a general shift away from research directed towards the needs of intensive, monocropping systems relying on the use of external chemical inputs.

Improving direct physical animal-to-crop contributions

The major direct physical contributions of the livestock sub-sector to that of crops are the provision of:

- draught power and;
- manure.

Where draught power has already been introduced the challenge is to improve its efficiency, but there are still many areas of the tropics where cultivation is still practised manually. These areas would benefit by the introduction of draught power. Where farmers are inexperienced in managing animals, this may prove more difficult than at first anticipated, requiring extensive institutional support in the form of credit, veterinary services and the like.

Draught power can increase crop output by expanding the area cultivated, by enabling a change in the cropping pattern, or by increasing yields. Where animal traction has been introduced, it appears to be the area effect that is most important. Several studies have shown that the average cultivated area is around 25 per cent greater on farms using animal draught than those not using it. In two-thirds of studies animal draught affected the cropping pattern, but only in 28 per cent of cases were yields per unit area increased.

If, indeed, it is in area cultivated that animal power has most to contribute then research and development efforts should concentrate on the timeliness and speed of cultivation. These can be improved not only by introducing better implements and harnesses but also by ensuring that draught animals are adequately fed and heavy enough to perform their duties at the critical period – the start of the rains when, after a long dry season, they are often at their weakest under traditional systems in which no supplementary feed is provided. Changes in land use patterns could be achieved through animal traction if it is used, for example, to improve drainage of heavy clay soils which cannot be cultivated by hand. Such drainage might also increase yields.

Animal manure is best used as a fertiliser in intensive systems. This is because such systems are likely to contain little land that is not cultivated, and so natural fallows can no longer be used to restore fertility naturally. Increasing the use of manure as a fertiliser can raise problems of labour availability.

Where there is currently little integration of animals with crops great care should be taken before the use of animal power or manure are considered. The availability of a potential reserve of animal power does not necessarily mean that its use will increase crop output. For example, the use of mouldboard ploughs on sand desert fulfills no agronomic purpose and may even delay sowing, which can be done very fast by a person dropping seeds into a hole made by a dibbing stick. In a short growing season, delay may be fatal.

Raising indirect animal-crop interactions through cash flow

The sale of animals and their products can provide cash for re-investment in the crop enterprise. The reverse is also true. And when earnings from one enterprise increase, this creates the opportunity to improve the inputs into the other. For instance, the increased sale of dairy produce may allow farmers to purchase improved seeds of staple crops. Indirect effects of this kind will be beneficial in systems where livestock are not well integrated with crops as well as in ones where they are.

Improving direct physical crop-to-animal contributions

The direct contributions of crops to the livestock enterprise are more important in well integrated systems than in those with spatial separation or distinct ownership of the two enterprises.

In integrated systems increases in crop production and the resulting greater availability of by-products as residues can be transferred immediately and directly to livestock. Monocrop research on cereals in the past concentrated on improving grain yields for human consumption at the expense of straw production. No account was taken of the feeding value and palatability of by-products as residues. More recently, these shortcomings have been corrected, at least in some research institutes. Where land is normally left fallow or considered as wasteland the possibility of cropping with fodder trees or forages, particularly leguminous and other species which fix nitrogen and thus improve the fertility of the soil, should be considered.

In systems with little integration, especially in extensive pastoral ones, the cost advantages of simply grazing naturally occurring species that are well adapted to local environmental conditions may outweigh any benefits accruing from attempts to improve the system by, for example, enriching natural pastures or feeding concentrate supplements, especially when these are risky investments in view of the high chances of drought. Exceptions to this general rule may lie in the creation of small-scale feed reserves in favoured areas such as wadi beds or where water collects in shallow depressions.

Bibliography

Ajayi, S.S. 1977. Live and carcass weights of giant rat *Cricetomys gambianus* Waterhouse and domestic rabbit *Oryctolagus cuniculus* L. *E. Afr. Wildl. J.* 15: pp. 223–227.

Bartholomew, P.W., Ly, R., Nantoume, N'G., Traoré, B., Khibé, T., Sissoko, K. and Naur, H. 1992. Dry-season cattle fattening by smallholder farmers in the semi-arid zone of Mali. *Afr. Livest. Res.* 2: pp. 21–38.

Barral, H., Bénéfice, E. and Boudet, G. 1983. *Systèmes de production d'élevage au Sénégal dans la région du Ferlo. Synthèse de fin d'études d'une équipe de recherches pluridisciplinaries (Etudes et Synthèses N° 8).* Institut d'Elevage et de Médecine Vétérinaire des Pays Tropicaux: Maisons-Alfort, France.

Bizimungu, A. 1986. *Productivité des petits ruminants en milieu rural. 1. Diagnostic de recensement-bétail dans trois régions différentes de la CEPGL.* Institut de Recherche Agronomique et Zootechnique: Gitega, Burundi.

Blair, G. and Lefroy, R. (eds). 1991. *Technologies for sustainable agriculture on marginal uplands in Southeast Asia (ACIAR Proceedings Series N° 33).* Australian Centre for International Agricultural Research: Canberra, Australia.

Bonnet, P. 1988. *Etude de l'élevage dans le développement des zones cotonnières (Ph.D. Thesis).* Université de Montpellier: Montpellier, France.

Bourzat, D. and Wilson, R.T. 1988. *Principaux aspects zootechniques de la production des petits ruminants dans les systèmes agro-pastoraux du Yatenga (Burkina Faso) (Etudes et Synthèses N° 31).* Institut d'Elevage et de Médecine Vétérinaire des Pays Tropicaux: Maisons-Alfort, France.

Coomans, P. and Gaullier, P. 1982. L'élevage bovin sous palmeraies au cameroun, gestion des troupeaux et des pâturages. *Productions animales au bénéfice de l'homme: colloque internationale.* Institut de Médecine Tropicale Prince Léopold: Anivers, Belgium. pp. 192–198.

Dasmann, R.F. 1964. *African game ranching.* Pergamon: Oxford, UK.

de Leeuw, P.N., Reynolds, L. and Rey, B. 1993. Nutrient transfers from livestock in West African agricultural production systems. Paper presented at a Conference on livestock and sustainable nutrient cycling in mixed farming systems in sub-saharan Africa. Addis Ababa, Ethiopia.

de Montgolfier-Kouevi, C. and Vlavanou, A. 1983. *Tendances et perspectives de l'agriculture et de l'élevage en Afrique sub-Saharienne (Rapport de recherche N° 1).* Centre International pour l'Elevage en Afrique (CIPEA): Addis Ababa, Ethiopia.

de Queiroz, J.S., Gutierrez-Aleman, N. and Ponce de León, F.A. 1986. The ecology and management of small ruminant production systems in the sertão of Ceara, in the northeast of Brazil. *Agric. Syst.* 22: pp. 259–287.

Delgado, C.L. 1979. *The southern Fulani farming system in Upper Volta: A model for the integration of crop and livestock production in the West African savannah (African*

Rural Economy Paper N° 20). African Rural Economy Program, Department of Agricultural Economics, Michigan State University: East Lansing, USA.

Devendra, C. (ed). 1987. *Small ruminant production systems in South and South-east Asia*. International Development Research Centre: Ottawa, Canada.

Epstein, H. 1971. *The origins of the domestic animals of Africa*. Africana Publishing Corporation: New York, USA.

FAO. 1985. *Farming snails*. Food and Agriculture Organisation: Rome, Italy.

FAO. 1988. *Production yearbook, Volume 42*. Food and Agriculture Organisation: Rome, Italy.

FAO. 1991. Issues and perspectives in sustainable agriculture and rural development (Main Document N° 1, FAO/Netherlands Conference on Agriculture and the Environment, 's-Hertogenbosch, The Netherlands, 15–19 April 1991). Food and Agriculture Organisation: Rome, Italy. (mimeo).

FAO. 1993. An operational classification of world livestock systems for the livestock-environment study. Food and Agriculture Organisation: Rome, Italy. (mimeo).

Fielding, D. 1991. *Rabbits*. The Tropical Agriculturalist, Macmillan/CTA: London, UK.

Francis, P.A. 1988. Ox draught power and agricultural transformation in northern Zambia. *Agric. Syst.* 24: pp. 35–49.

Gatenby, R.M. 1991. *Sheep*. The Tropical Agriculturalist, Macmillan/CTA: London, UK.

Gibson, T. 1987. Northeast Thailand: A ley farming system using dairy cattle in the infertile uplands. *World Anim. Rev.* 61: pp. 36–43.

Gill, M., Owen, E., Pollott, G.E. and Lawrence, T.L.J. 1993. *Animal production in developing countries (Occasional Publication No 16)*. British Society of Animal Production: Edinburgh, UK.

Gips, T. 1986. What is sustainable agriculture? In: Allen P. and van Dusen, D. (eds), *Global perspectives on agroecology and sustainable agricultural systems (Proceedings of the 6th International Scientific Conference of the International Federation of Organic Agriculture Movements)*. Agroecology Program, University of California: Santa Cruz, USA. 1: pp. 63–74.

Grisley, W. 1993. Sustainable intensification of agricultural land use systems considering proper use of resources while avoiding environmental damage. Food and Agriculture Organisation: Rome, Italy. (mimeo).

Gryseels, G. 1988. *Role of livestock on mixed smallholder farms in the Ethiopian Highlands. A case study from the Baso and Worena wereda near Debre Berhan (Ph.D. Thesis)*. Agricultural University: Wageningen, The Netherlands.

Holness, D.H. 1991. *Pigs*. The Tropical Agriculturalist, Macmillan/CTA: London, UK.

Jalaludin, S. 1989. Ruminant feeding systems in Southeast Asia. In: *Feeding strategies for improving productivity of ruminant livestock in Developing Countries (Panel Proceedings Series STI/PUB/823)*. International Atomic Energy Agency: Vienna, Austria: pp. 31–50.

Kolff, H.E. and Wilson, R.T. 1985. Livestock production in central Mali: The 'Mouton de case' system of smallholder sheep fattening. *Agric. Syst.* 16: pp. 217–230.

Landais, E. 1983. *Analyse des systèmes d'élevage bovin sédebtaire du nord de la Côte d'Ivoire (Etudes et Synthèses N° 9)*. Institut d'Elevage et de Médecine Vétérinaire des Pays Tropicaux: Maison-Alfort, France.

Landais, E. and Faye, J. 1986. *Méthodes pour la recherche sur les systémes d'élevage en Afrique intertropicale (Etudes et Synthèses N° 20)*. Institut d'Elevage et de Médecine Vétérinaire des Pays Tropicaux: Maisons-Alfort, France.

Lebas, F., Coudert, P., Rouvier, R. and de Rochambeau, H. 1986. *The rabbit. Husbandry, health, production*. Food and Agriculture Organisation: Rome, Italy.

Leng, R.A., Preston, T.R., Sansoucy, R. and Kunju, G.P.J. 1991. Multinutrient blocks as a strategic supplement for ruminants. *World Anim. Rev.* 67: pp. 11–20.

Leyva, V. 1989. Sistemas de producción de alpacas. In: *Simposio producción de alpacas y llamas (XII Reunion Científica Anual de la Asociación Peruana de Producción Animal)*. Universidad Nacional Mayor de San Marcos: Lima, Peru: pp. 157–174.

Lhoste, P. 1987. *L'association agriculture-élevage. Evolution du système agropastoral au Siné Saloum (Sénégal) (Etudes et Synthèses N° 21)*. Institut d'Elevage et de Médecine Vétérinaire des Pays Tropicaux: Maisons-Alfort, France.

Liang, J.B., Nasir, A.M., Ismail, A. and Abdullah, R.S. 1989. Management of draught animals in Malaysian oil palm estates. In: Hoffmann, D., Nari, J. and Petheram, R.J. (eds), *Draught animals in rural development*. Australian Centre for International Agricultural Research: Canberra, Australia: pp. 242–245.

Ly, C. 1993. L'étable fumière: voie d'intensification de l'élevage. Projet Régional RAF/88/100: Banjul, The Gambia.

Mason, I.L. (ed). 1984. *Evolution of domesticated animals*. Longman: London, UK.

Matthewman, R.W. 1994. *Dairying*. The Tropical Agriculturalist, Macmillan/CTA: London, UK.

McDowell, R.E. and Hilderbrand, P.E. 1980. *Integrated crop and animal production: Making the most of resources available to small farms in developing countries*. The Rockefeller Foundation: Washington DC, USA.

McIntire, J., Bourzat, D. and Pingali P. 1992. *Crop-livestock interaction in sub-Saharan Africa*. World Bank: Washington DC, USA.

Monod, T. 1975. *Pastoralism in tropical Africa*. Clarendon Press: Oxford, UK.

Msellati, L. (ed). 1993. *Elevage sous cocoteraies: Intégration et diversification – exemple du Vanatu*. CIRAD–EMVT: Maisons-Alfort, France.

National Research Council. 1991. *Microlivestock. Little-known small animals with a promising economic future*. BOSTID, National Academy Press: Washington DC, USA.

Nordblom, T.L., Ahmed, A.K.H. and Potts, G.R. 1985. *Research methodology for livestock on-farm trials*. International Development Research Centre: Ottawa, Canada.

Norman, D. and Collinson, M. 1985. Farming systems research in theory and practice. In: *Agricultural systems research for developing countries (Proceedings Series N° 11)*. Australian Council for International Agricultural Research: Canberra, Australia.

Norse, D. 1992. The global context: Sharing the world's resources. In: Marshall, B.J. (ed), *Sustainable livestock farming into the 21st century (CAS Paper N° 25)*. Centre for Agricultural Strategy, University of Reading: Reading, UK.

Okali, C. and Sumberg, J.E. 1985. Sheep and goats, men and women: Household relations and small ruminant development in southwest Nigeria. *Agric. Syst.* 18: pp. 39–58.

Patanik, S. and Ramakrishnan, P.S. 1989. Comparative study of energy flow through village ecosystems in two co-existing communities (the Khasis and the Nepalis) of Meghalaya in north-east India. *Agric. Syst.* 30: 245–265.

Petheram, R.J. 1986. *A farming systems approach to ruminant research in Java (Ph.D. Thesis)*. University of New England: Armidale, Australia.

Pingali, P., Bigot, Y. and Binswanger, H.P. 1987. *Agricultural mechanization and the evolution of farming systems in sub-Saharan Africa*. Johns Hopkins University Press: Baltimore, USA.

Powell, J.M. 1986. Manure for cropping: A case study from central Nigeria. *Expt. Agric.* 22: pp. 15–24.

Ruthenberg, H. 1980. *Farming systems in the tropics (3rd edition)*. Clarendon Press: Oxford, UK.

Saadullah, M. and Das, S.C. 1987. Integrated crop and small ruminant systems in Bangladesh. In: Devendra, C. (ed), *Small ruminant production systems in South and South-east Asia*. International Development Research Centre: Ottawa, Canada: pp. 203–222.

Schwartz, H.J. 1983. Improved utilization of arid rangelands through multiple species herds. *Proc. 5th. World Conf. Anim. Prod.* 2: pp. 625–626.

Setioko, A.R., Evans, A.J. and Raharjo, Y.C. 1985. Productivity of herded ducks in West Java. *Agric. Syst.* 16: pp. 1–5.

Smith, A.J. 1990. *Poultry*. The Tropical Agriculturalist, Macmillan/CTA: London, UK.

Smith, A.J. 1992. Priorities and options for livestock production in developing countries. *Outlook Agric.* 21: pp. 13–19.

Smith, A.J. and Gunn, R.G. 1979. *Intensive animal production in developing countries (Occasional Publication No 4)*. British Society of Animal Production: Edinburgh, UK.

Spedding, C.R.W. 1985. *An introduction to agricultural systems (2nd edition)*. Applied Science: London, UK.

Thomson, E.F. and Bahhady, F. 1986. *Aspects of sheep husbandry systems in Aleppo province of north west Syria (Research Report N° 16)*. International Center for Agricultural Research in the Dry Areas: Aleppo, Syria.

Ucko, P.J. and Dimbleby, G.W. (eds). 1969. *The domestication and exploitation of plants and animals*. Duckworth: London, UK.

Upton, M. 1985. Returns from small ruminant production in south west Nigeria. *Agric. Syst.* 17: pp. 65–83.

van Soest, P.J. 1982. *Nutritional ecology of the ruminant*. O & B Books: Corvallis, USA.

Wilson, R.T. 1986. Mixed species stocking and the vital statistics and demography of domestic animals in the arid and semi-arid zones of northern tropical Africa. In: Joss, P.J., Lynch, P.W. and Williams, O.B. (eds), *Rangelands: A resource under siege*. Australian Academy of Science: Canberra, Australia: pp. 375–378.

Wilson, R.T. 1988. Small ruminant production systems in tropical Africa. *Small Rumin. Res.* 1: pp. 305–25.

Wilson, R.T., Bailey, L., Hales, J., Moles, D. and Watkins, A.E. 1980. The cultivation-cattle complex in Western Darfur. *Agric. Syst.* 5: pp. 119–135.

Wilson, R.T. and Clarke, S.E. 1975. Studies on the livestock of Southern Darfur, Sudan. I. The ecology and livestock resources of the area. *Trop. Anim. Hlth. Prod.* 7: pp. 165–187.

Wilson, R.T., de Leeuw, P.N. and de Haan, C. 1983. *Recherches sur les systèmes en zones arides: Résultats preliminaires (Rapport de recherche N° 5)*. International Livestock Centre for Africa: Addis Ababa, Ethiopia.

Zeuner, F.E. 1963. *A history of domesticated animals*. Hutchinson: London, UK.

Index